CW01024055

Research Papers in

Luke Gibbons's *Gaelic Gothic* is the second in an occasional series of research papers commissioned by the Centre for Irish Studies at NUI, Galway. The series is designed to bring the most innovative research in Irish Studies to as broad an audience as possible, and to provide, by its excellence and diversity, a model for the future development of the discipline.

In the first publication of this series, *Hidden Ireland, Public Sphere*, Joep Leerssen charted the cultural process by which native Irish culture emerged from the oppressive cultural segregation of the eighteenth century under the Penal Laws to form part of the burgeoning nationalist public sphere in the nineteenth century. This was the story of the Catholic, Gaelic-speaking population coming in from the margins, and playing the central role in the making of modern Ireland. But what were the forces that pushed the native Irish to the margins in the first place? On what grounds were a Catholic or Gaelic-speaking population considered unfit for civil society and modernity? In this new study, *Gaelic Gothic* Luke Gibbons argues that the anti-Catholic animus (hostility) of the Gothic genre in the eighteenth century merged with new concepts of racial inferiority to exclude the Irish from the modern world. In keeping with the demonology of the Gothic, the threat presented by the Irish had less to do with visibility than with *invisibility*, but was no less racially grounded for that. Instead of skin colour, the dominant biological markers of 'the Celt' were associated with disease and collective contagion. Originally physical, this contagion passed imperceptibly into notions of political contagion, as the Irish capacity for infiltrating and combating White Anglo-Saxon Protestant ideals of racial supremacy challenged the very basis of the cultural logic of colonialism.

The Centre for Irish Studies was established at NUI, Galway in 2000 and is dedicated to research and advanced teaching on the cultural, social, and political endeavours of Irish people on the island of Ireland and beyond. Details of the Centre's programmes in teaching and research are available on our website at: www.nuigalway.ie/research/centre_irish_studies/

For Tadhg Foley

GAELIC GOTHIC

race, colonization, and irish culture

Luke Gibbons

ARLEN
HOUSE

First published by Arlen House in June 2004

Arlen House
PO Box 222
Galway
Ireland
arlenhouse@ireland.com

ISBN   1–903631–39–4 paperback

Editorial: Centre for Irish Studies, NUI, Galway
Cover Design: Sean Mannion
Typesetting: Arlen House
Printed by: ColourBooks, Baldoyle, Dublin 13

CONTENTS

ILLUSTRATIONS

Gaelic Gothic

1 INTRODUCTION: RACE, RELIGION, AND THE GOTHIC

> Every people in every age have had their country of
> monsters, where the human kind, like evil demons,
> drink human blood, and live on the marrow of dead
> men's bones ... Mrs Anne Radcliffe being dead ... it is
> now our part to furnish England with monsters,
> thugs, and 'devils great and devils small.'
>
> - 'Priest-Hunting,' *The Nation*, 5 February 1848

Writing in 1646 against the backdrop of an imminent Cromwellian conquest of Ireland, the Rev Hugh Peters [Fig. 1], one of the most avid Puritan propagandists, recommended short shrift for Irish papists.

Fig. 1: Rev Hugh Peters

Drawing on a seven-year stay in America, he proposed that 'the wild *Irish* and the *Indian* doe not much differ, and therefore would be handled alike' – namely, through the implementation of a scorched-earth policy that would not 'spend time about Castles and Forts' but would 'burne up the Enemies provisions every where'.[1] Peters probably had in mind the destruction of Indian settlements in Virginia (1622-32) and Connecticut (1636-37),[2] but these in turn were part of a colonial mentality that had used slash-and-burn tactics to devastating effect during the late Elizabethan conquest of Ireland. 'Till Ireland can be famished it can not be subdued', wrote Edmund Spenser to Queen Elizabeth, and her deputies in Ireland, Lord Mountjoy and Lord Carew, took him fatefully at his word.[3] Peters himself took part in the implementation of such policies, advocating mass transportation of the Irish poor to Barbados and, as Cromwell's chaplain, acting as one of his closest advisors on his campaign of massacre and pillage throughout Ireland.[4] Though extermination was the logic of such practices, it is striking how much religion and race were intertwined in this early period so that Indians were vilified not only as tawny brutes but as wicked heathens, while the Irish were condemned as much for their degenerate savagery as for their Popish superstitions. As racial discourse assumed its more recognizable biological manifestations in the eighteenth and nineteenth centuries, it is not surprising that its previous religious and ethnic/cultural components gave way to more clear-cut epidermal schemas of colour and visual difference. Yet, as the persistence of anti-Semitism shows, skin pigmentation did not exhaust the complexities of race, and religious intolerance and colonial habits of authority, with their less conspicuous freight of sectarianism and ethnocentrism, were never entirely abandoned.

In what follows, I will argue that, as the arteries of modern racial discourse began to harden into notions of blood and belonging, the Gothic as a mode of sensibility took on board much of its cultural pathology, maintaining a series of deep-seated, troubled connections with wider systems of prejudice, paranoia, and bigotry. Though originally a literary genre, with a distinctively popular or sensational appeal, the Gothic spread out into the recesses of everyday life, giving rise to a phantom public sphere haunted by fear, terror, and the dark side of civility.[5] The Gothic in this sense can be seen as following through the cultural work of the Glorious Revolution of 1688-91, expunging the traces not only of feudalism but also its archaic Catholic remnants from the social order. Hence the familiar stage-props of the Gothic *mise-en-scene*: ruined castles, predatory aristocrats, silhouetted graveyards, fragmented manuscripts or wills, mouldering abbeys and monasteries, endless, hidden vaults and torture chambers, lecherous monks and nuns – with the victims taking the form of virtuous maidens or metropolitan 'sophisticates' at odds with the unresolved legacies of the past or present-day colonies. Though often set in Italy or Spain, or in other vestiges of medieval Christendom, it was not just Catholicism that came back from the grave: 'primitive' or pre-modern cultures provided their own revenants, as entire societies and various 'doomed races' became the anthropological equivalents of the architectural ruins that scarred the landscape.

Much has been written about the threat presented by Catholicism and residual Jacobitism to the formation of 'Britishness' in the eighteenth century, as if the issues in contention were primarily those of religious tolerance, and the difficulties presented by Catholic emancipation. For Linda Colley, the 'Catholic other' – located mainly in the absolutist regimes of France – was rendered redundant by the French Revolution, and was superceded with the expansion of empire in the nineteenth century by a new exotic, racial other in the outer reaches of empire. This fails to acknowledge that race and empire begin at home, and that both colonization and the animus against Catholicism were inherently bound up with the subjugation of the Celtic periphery – Gaelic Ireland and the Scottish Highlands – from the early modern period.[6] As David Armitage has shown, the forging of the unity of the 'Three Kingdoms' was not antecedent to colonial expansion but was intrinsic to it, with Ireland's strategic position in the Atlantic placing it at once both inside and outside the domestic boundaries of Britain. 'The language of civility and barbarism', moreover, was not restricted to religion but was 'mapped onto the divide between Celtic and non-Celtic', leading James IV, for example, to use the language of colonization even for the purpose of reclaiming territories within Scotland for the project of civility.[7] As LP Curtis has pointed out, Anglocentric historians have tended to disregard issues of race, ethnicity, or colonization when dealing with the Irish question or 'internal colonialism', but:

> cling instead to the more academically respectable charge of anti-Catholicism, which somehow seems less reprehensible owing to its Tudor-Stuart lineage. By concentrating on the sectarian or religious component in anti-Irish prejudice, they are able to argue that Irish Catholics in Britain bore no burden of prejudice beyond what every other Catholic in the United Kingdom had to endure by way of 'papist' stigma.[8]

But, in fact, Irish Catholicism was of a very different order than its more courtly English counterparts, whether of the Royalist Jacobite variety or the later refined Oxford movement. From the time of the Norman Conquest, notions of degeneracy were associated with Ireland, then at the edge of the known world, as in the imputations of cannibalism, incest, and bloodletting that provided an alibi for the conquest in Giraldus Cambrensis's *Topographia Hibernia* (c.1185). It might have been expected that imputations of Irish savagery would diminish when it was overtaken by the utter strangeness of the New World, but this was not the case.[9] In the writings of Edmund Spenser, Swift, and down to the modern period of the Great Famine, the association between famine, cannibalism, and the desperation of the Irish loomed large in the colonial imagination. According to George Stocking, the rise of anthropology as a science itself bore witness to 'a close articulation, both experiential and ideological, between the domestic and colonial spheres of otherness',[10] an argument given a further, local habitation by HL Malchow:

> One needs, however, to ground this articulation more firmly in a deeper popular culture that had long invested the outsider, particularly the Celtic outsider, with a demonic, primitive and dangerous aspect. Popular responsiveness to the racialization of cultural difference by the mid-Victorian

intelligentsia had its roots, not only in the conjunction of social-evolutionist ideas, colonial expansion, and the creation of an urban industrial proletariat, but in folk myth and long standing domestic prejudice directed against gypsies, Jews, and, especially in England, Celtic vagabonds.[11]

The otherness of Irish Catholicism thus possessed an ineradicable ethnic component, being perceived as immersed in superstition, savagery, and the general credulousness associated with primitive cultures or 'doomed races'. As *Punch* expressed it with characteristic understatement in an 'Ode to the Irish Elections' during the cataclysm of the Famine in 1848:

How's the nose by which you're led
Like a stupid quadraped (sic)?
Six foot PADDY, are you no bigger –
You, whom cozening friars dish –
Mentally than the poorest nigger
Grovelling before fetish?

You to Sambo I compare
Under superstition's rule
Prostrate like an abject fool.[12]

As if to remove the taint of superstition and ethnic inferiority, Irish Catholicism itself, through the post-Famine 'Devotional Revolution', sought to distance itself as much as possible from the 'primitive' vernacular base which had sustained it during the Penal Laws. Through an accommodation with Victorian values, it pursued an extensive social reconstruction programme based on education and health initiatives, church-building, and a pursuit of respectability consistent with the emergence of middle-class constitutional nationalism. Not least of the ironies here was that an anxiety over its despised pre-Famine roots played no small part in the vigorous expansion of Irish missionary activity in the twentieth century, the determination to purge superstition and primitivism at home leading to a similar intolerance of any kind of indigenous practices or local beliefs that might add to the white man's burden in the colonies.[13]

There is little doubt that the original preoccupation with Catholicism in the Gothic genre – as exemplified by Horace Walpole, Ann Radcliffe, or Matthew Lewis – was animated by a belief in the persistence of the Old Regime, whether abroad in absolutist France or, more to the point, at home in the Gaelic outposts of Britain and Ireland. From this perspective, the terror of the French Revolution and the ferocity with which it swept away the pomp and wealth of the Catholic Church could be seen as the acceleration of the Gothic in action, and was welcomed as such by British radicals such as Richard Price and Joseph Priestly. It was readily apparent from the outset, however, that more than religion was at stake in this purging of the old order, and that the kind of monarchical power and aristocratic privileges left in place in Britain by the Glorious Revolution were also in its sights. Not least of Edmund Burke's rhetorical achievements in *Reflections on the Revolution in France* (1790) was to launch a powerful counter-offensive against the conventional Gothic, shifting the locus of terror from the ancient to the modern, from Jacobite to Jacobin. On this scheme of things, it was the remnants of the old order – including the Catholic Church – who were the *victims* of terror, thereby construing the aggrandizement of the Jacobins under the sign of modernity as the new monsters of the Gothic imagination.[14] Though directed primarily at events in France, this had far-reaching implications for the Catholic cause in Ireland, to which Burke had devoted much of his career: if the Catholic population here was also on the receiving end, the monster could only be the oppressive Protestant Ascendancy that arrogated all power to itself, depriving the mass of the Irish population of their most basic liberties. As Francophobia gathered pace in England, it was convenient to ascribe the carnage on the streets of Paris to the deviancy of the French national character, but Burke, with a Gothic narrative twist, brought the sins of the fathers back to base. The inspiration for the mainstream anti-Catholic Gothic may have been the Glorious Revolution, but the ghoulish ancestry of the new republican Gothic could be traced to its more ruthless precursor, the murderous excesses of Cromwell and his minions. Chief among these for Burke was none other than the Rev Hugh Peters, the most vociferous proponent of regicide, but also of genocide: the avenging angel who had advocated extermination of the Irish and Indians in the 1630s was now unmasked as the monster himself. In the *Reflections*, Burke countered Richard Price's attempt to legitimize the French Revolution by linking it to the Glorious Revolution, proposing instead that it be traced to an earlier primal scene:

> when a predecessor of Dr. Price, the Reverend Hugh Peters, made the vault of the King's own chapel at St. James's ring with the honours and privileges of the Saints who, with the 'high praises of God in their mouths, and a *two-edged* sword in their hands, were to execute judgment on the heathen, and punishments upon the *people*, to bind their *kings* with chains, and their *nobles* with fetters of iron.[15]

In Burke's hands, the Gothic itself became a two-edged sword, but not always in the way that he imagined. Though the genre carried much of the paranoia of racial discourse, it was still a *genre*, and unlike its immutable biological counterpart, was subject to historical change and human intervention. Though sharing – indeed partly constituting – the demonology of race, the Gothic as a literary and cultural form could be turned, through acts of semiotic and narrative appropriation, against itself, thereby becoming a weapon of the weak. It is true that under colonization, one strand of the Cromwellian legacy in Ireland maintained a perpetual ascendancy over the subjugated Catholic population, but a contrasting radical current in Protestant republicanism, inspired by the United Irishman, sought to align itself with

Cromwell oppression of Irish Catholics
Anglo-Irish support of " "
(United Irishmen)

repressing the quality

both the Catholic and Gaelic cause, thereby fomenting an anti-colonial politics that went beyond Burke's critique of modernity. As we shall see, by vitiating the regressive nostalgia of Celticism itself as a proto-racist ideology, radical counter-currents in Irish culture launched a pre-emptive strike against the lethal intersection of the Gothic with new, biological conceptions of race in the nineteenth century. For all its grounding in biology, race is also a *discourse*, and much of its rhetorical shrillness derives from its buried cultural genealogy in genres such as the Gothic. By redressing rather than disavowing the sins of the past, Gaelic Gothic rattled the skeletons in its own vaults, thus going some way towards exposing the calcified cultural deposits that underlie the ideology of race itself.

2 JACOBITE GENEALOGIES

> Next to the gothic in point of sublimity and
> imagination comes the Celtic ... This superstition,
> like the gothic . . . does not, like most mythological
> systems, involve every species of absurdity, but
> floating loose upon the mind, founds its imagery
> upon a metaphysical possibility, upon the
> appearance of superior, or departed beings.
>
> - Nathan Drake, 'On Gothic Superstition' (1798)

Though the Gothic did not emerge fully-fledged as a genre
until 1764 with the publication of Horace Walpole's *The Castle
of Otranto*, elements of the genre had already featured in the
literary canon, most notably in representations of ghosts,
apparitions, or other manifestations of the supernatural. As
Rolf Loeber and Magda Stouthammer-Loeber point out,
Gothic motifs were a notable feature of two novels published
in Dublin before Walpole's novel, the anonymous *The
Adventure of Miss Sophia Berkley* (1760), and *Longsword, Earl of
Salisbury* (1762), written by the eminent Trinity College
historian, Thomas Leland, which displayed a particular
penchant for nefarious friars and feudal despotism.[16] The fear
of Catholic, not to mention Jacobite, resurgence was never far
from overheated Protestant imaginations in Britain in the mid-
eighteenth century, and was responsible for the episode in
Henry Fielding's *Tom Jones* (1749) which gives us one of the
earliest glimpses of the Gothic. In this episode, Tom brings the
gullible Jacobite Partridge to a production of *Hamlet* on the
London stage, and is both bemused and taken aback when
Partridge is overwhelmed by David Garrick's performance
during the ghost scene. Garrick's mastery of his role is so
compelling that Partridge is convinced the ghost of Hamlet's

father is real – 'and fell into so violent a trembling, that his knees knocked against each other'. When asked about Garrick's acting, however, Partridge denies the great tragedian was acting at all, adding disingenuously that 'I am sure if I had seen a ghost, I should have looked in the very same manner, and done just as he did'. By contrast, Partridge singles out the performance of the actor who played the King for special praise, for there, he argues, is a real pretender on the throne, as is particularly evident during the dumb-show scene: 'A good actor, and doth all he can to hide it . . . . No wonder he runs away; for your sake, I'll never trust an innocent face again'.[17]

For all Partridge's naiveté, and the note of ridicule in Fielding's treatment of him, the Jabobite resonances of this scene are not too difficult to discern: the spectral return of a deposed monarch to warn his son about a usurper on the throne, and his son's impending doom, could not have failed to strike a chord with Jacobite sympathizers in the aftermath of Culloden.[18] These sympathies were far removed from Fielding's own political views, which had more in common with the different rendering of the primal scene of usurpation and guilt that forms the basis of Walpoles's *The Castle of Ortanto*. Walpole's father, Sir Robert Walpole, was perhaps the politician who did most to counter the Jacobite threat and secure the Hanoverian succession in the early decades of the eighteenth century, and from what is known of his son's allegiances, there is little doubt that Manfred, the usurper who steals the throne in the novel, is meant to evoke James II, the corrupter of the ancient constitution. According to the Whig interpretation, the Glorious Revolution did not constitute a radical break with the past so much as an act of restoration, the re-instatement of the rightful heir to the kingdom after the temporary interruption of the Protestant succession. Yet, as Robert Miles argues, the matter is not as simple as that in *The Castle of Otranto*, for the tyrant Manfred is deposed through the offices of a monk, Father Jerome, whose son Theodore –

Glorious Rev: When pro Catholic James II was deposed/abdicated for William of orange & Mary — Prots!

the peasant unmasked as a prince – subsequently ascends to the throne. What is at stake here is unresolved guilt and the question of legitimacy, several generations after the event – 'a much deeper anxiety, one feeding the Gothic genre in general: the fear that the post-Glorious Revolution settlement is without legitimacy'.[19] While there were more general questions surrounding legitimacy without divine sanction or transcendental grounding in an emergent constitutional monarchy, the anxieties at the core of the Gothic were also generated by a series of troubling contradictions nearer to hand: that liberty and civil society in Britain could only be maintained by the despotism and terror of colonialism, beginning with the Celtic periphery. As John Locke's response to his friend William Molyneux's *The Case of Ireland Stated* (1698) made clear as early as the 1690s, government through consent in Britain required withholding it from Ireland, even in the case of a Protestant parliament. So far from relegating tyranny and oppression to the past, the Whig settlement was doomed to repeat it in the present, albeit at a spatial remove in colonial territories. While the Jacobite ghost had been politically exorcized in the decades after Culloden, it assumed a new, cultural afterlife in the Irish and Scottish periphery, re-emerging in the national imaginaries of Ossian, Celticism, the historical novel, and, of course, the Gothic itself.

Hence the facility with which depictions of Ireland and the Scottish Highlands as the last outposts of savagery and superstition lent themselves to some of the earliest forays into the Gothic, before the more canonical fusions of the genre with 'the National Tale' in the early 1800s.[20] As Siobhan Kilfeather notes, many of the ominous landmarks of the Gothic already featured in representations of the Celtic periphery, the tumultuous storm crossing the Irish sea in Elizabeth Griffith's early *The History of Lady Barton* (1771), for example, setting the scene for much of what was to follow:

> [From] the influence of Burke's *Philosophical Enquiry into the Origin of our Ideas of the Sublime and Beautiful* (1757), and into

early gothic scenes in the novels of Frances Sheridan and Elizabeth Griffith, one may trace a continuity between the uses of 'wild' Ireland in the poetry and romance of Spenser and Milton, the mystification of Celtic landscapes by mid-eighteenth-century poets such as Gray and Macpherson, as well as in travel narratives, and the exploitation of the Celtic 'fringes' in the earliest setting for gothic passages in fiction. Such an examination reveals Ireland to be one of the original sites of the gothic, and may help to explain the status of Ireland as a gothic scene in the nineteenth-century.[21]

Ann Radcliffe's first attempt at the genre, *The Castles of Athlin and Dunbayne* (1789), took up the theme of usurpation from *The Castle of Otranto* but projected it into the wilds of Scotland, and the Highlands were also the setting for Sophia Lee's earlier *The Recess* (1780), another melodrama of damaged inheritance, and John Palmer's *The Haunted Cavern: A Caledonian Tale* (1796).[22] In 1773, the Scottish setting of *Macbeth* moved from being a mere backdrop when it was staged in tartan costume, reclaiming another story of usurpation, complete with its Gothic trappings of ghosts and witches, for the tradition of the Highlands.[23] Scotland also provided the stage for the first dramatic enactment of the vampire myth, JR Planche's *The Vampire; or, The Bride of the Isles* (1820). The first Gothic revival castle was built at Inveraray (1746-1758) by the Duke of Argyle 'to awe the Scottish peasantry after the 1745 Jacobite rebellion' – a model which was then imitated, as Rupert Davenport-Hines points out, by the Protestant Ascendancy in Ireland, particularly after the 1798 rebellion. It is no coincidence that it was the same Duke who is most identified with the subsequent outlawing of the Gaelic language, clan tartans, and pipes from the Scottish public sphere.[24]

The association of the Gothic genre with the outlying Gaelic fastnesses of Britain coincided with a period in which 'the enemy within' was reincarnated as a force of pity and terror: the fighting Irish or the ferocious Highlanders who became the cutting edge of the imperial army. It is for this reason that genocide was never really on the cards, for, despite the revulsion towards 'popery', the Gaelic language, and clan society, the able-bodied male was too valuable as a foot-soldier, or as a menial labourer, in strengthening the sinews of empire. Purged from the civil sphere, the Celt became a contradictory amalgam of tenderness and terror, sentiment and savagery – human society, in fact, reduced to its most elemental, primitive condition. In tandem with this Jekyll and Hyde persona, the Celt also began to enjoy a new twilit existence in the realms of the aesthetic, passing out of public life into the desolate, elegiac landscapes of the Ossian poems, first sprung on an unsuspecting public by James Macpherson in the early 1760s. In the Ossianic cycle, the warrior culture of the Scottish Highlands was rehabilitated for the metropolitan reading public of London and, indeed, of Europe and the US, by locating it in a distant past, safely removed from the exigencies of the present. What is seldom appreciated in accounts of the cult of Ossian is the link with the Gothic investment in terror, the need for a shattered culture to redeem its honour and wounded pride on the battlefields of empire. The Ossian controversy, the rise of the Gothic novel, and the development of the aesthetics of terror in Edmund Burke's landmark *Enquiry into the Sublime and Beautiful* (1757), all coincide with the Seven Years War in America and India, and the unprecedented expansion of the British Empire. In an important sense, the Ossianic poems, and the ideology of the sighing, warlike Celt which they engendered, can be seen as an aesthetic call to arms, preparing the injured masculinity of the 'Celtic races' for what lay in store for them in America, Africa or India. 'They went forth to the war, *but they always fell*', wrote Macpherson, in what became for Matthew Arnold a valedictory credo for Celticism itself in the Victorian era.[25]

Thus, while the recourse to the consolations of poetry mitigated the threat of the enemy within by removing him in time to a remote past, the imperial, military project removed him to an equally remote location in space, to the outreaches – or frontiers – of empire. The denial of civility or democracy to the Irish polity noted above in relation to Locke was in keeping with the need to maintain the Celt as a fighting machine – so long as his violence was placed in the service of empire. Military discipline, not surprisingly, was considered the most appropriate means of keeping this violence in check and, in effect, became the norm for civil society itself in Ireland under martial law and the innumerable insurrection acts of the late eighteenth and nineteenth centuries. It is not, therefore, as if the Celtic proclivity for violence were 'pre-modern', an anachronism from a clan system out of place in the refined moral ambience of the imperial centre. As Sir Walter Scott wrote in his introduction to *Rob Roy*, part of the fascination with the famous outlaw lay in the fact that he was not an anachronism, but a contemporary, performing such feats:

> in the beginning of the 18th century, as are usually ascribed to Robin Hood in the middle ages, - and that within forty miles of Glasgow, a great commercial city, the seat of a learned university. Thus a character like his, blending the wild virtues, the subtle policy, and unrestrained license of an American Indian, was flourishing during the Augustan Age of Queen Anne and George I.[26]

Scott goes on to suggest that it is this 'strong contrast' between civility and savagery which excites our interest, but as Ian Duncan has argued, it is not just the contrast but the *connection* between the two that animates the action in the novel: 'Despite their official opposition, savagery and commerce sustain rather than cancel one another, constituting a dark, intricate kind of present'.[27] Among objectors to Ossian, some of the most caustic criticisms concerned the historical sleight of hand whereby the civility of the present was projected back onto ancient 'Celtic' society, as if the two could co-exist in the same sphere. As

John Pinkerton, the most acerbic critic of Celticism, expressed it:

> Of the pretended poems of Ossian, the son of this Fin, it is almost beneath the purpose of this work to speak ... As to us in Scotland, foreigners seem, on this occasion, justly to question whether we be savages or not. For that the most civilized and benevolent manners should belong to savage society, as represented in Ossian, is not so absurd as that such a delusion should impose on any, in a country advanced beyond a savage state ... Certain it is, that had those poems of Ossian been published by an Irishman, all Scotland, from the Mull of Galloway to the Orkneys, would have been in one peal of laughter at so enormous a bull.[28]

It is difficult not to suspect that the real fear is of the reverse process, whereby the savagery of the Irish infiltrates – indeed, is produced by – modernity. Extending this to the Gothic genre, with its rogues gallery of monks, nuns, and lecherous aristocrats, it would seem that the cruelty, barbarism, and superstition which the Whig imagination ascribed to the middle ages were as much disavowed components of its own culture, as it resorted to, and incorporated, the methods of 'the enemy' to maintain its hold on empire. What is the autocratic nature of colonial rule in Ireland or India, Edmund Burke suggested, but absolutism in disguise, the superceded tyranny of the Middle Ages re-appearing in modern form? Hence Charles Maturin's explanation, in the preface to his novel, *The Milesian Chief* (1812), as to why Ireland was pre-eminently suitable as a setting for Gothic fictions:

> I have chosen my country for the scene, because I believe it is the only country on earth, where ... the extremes of refinement and barbarism are united, and the most wild and incredible situations of romantic story are hourly passing before modern eyes.[29]

The most optimistic reading of this would have it that 'barbarism' and the 'wild' are archaic residues of a doomed social order, soon be to be replaced by the forces of civility and refinement: but the less benign reading, that shared by Maturin himself, sees barbarism as intrinsic to the maintenance of colonial rule, not simply a transient phase in the initial phase of conquest or 'primitive accumulation'. In this version of Gothic, the sins of the past become part of the underside of modernity itself as it weighs upon the minds of the living.

3 THE INVISIBLE HAND:
SUPERSTITION AND THE SUPERNATURAL

> These are then (the vulgar gothic and the Celtic) the
> only two species of superstition which are still
> likely to retain their ground; founded chiefly on the
> casual interference of immaterial beings, and
> therefore easily combining with the common
> feelings of humanity, they may yet with propriety
> decorate the pages of the poet.
>
> - Nathan Drake, 'On Gothic Superstition' (1798)

If the staging of the ghost scene in Garrick's *Hamlet*
represents an early conjunction of Jacobitism and the Gothic,
then another emanation of Hamlet's ghost provides one of
the gateways into the underworld of Irish Gothic. When
Hamlet is confronted by the apparition of his father on the
battlements of Elsinore, he is alarmed into reflection on the
ghost's origins, but immediately takes offence at Horatio's
questioning of the message from beyond the grave:

HORATIO: There's no offence, my Lord.
HAMLET: Yes, by St Patrick, but there is, Horatio. And
            much more offence too. Touching this vision
            here, It is an honest ghost, that let me tell
            you.[30]

As Stephen Greenblatt has acutely observed, the invocation
of St Patrick here raises a spectre that Protestant reformers
sought assiduously to exorcize in the early modern period.[31]
This concerned belief in purgatory and, by extension, its
suffering, restless souls: ghosts, spirits, and others doomed
to walk the earth. Crucially, purgatory was not an ethereal,
undiscovered country, but, to the medieval imagination

could be entered through various mysterious thresholds on the earth's surface. The most famous of these was St Patrick's Purgatory at Lough Derg, in the northwest of Ireland, and it is for this reason that, before the discovery of America, Ireland became the outer edge of the known world, a liminal zone between the natural and supernatural. Here, through a dark, foreboding cave, pilgrims could enter the vestibule of the underworld and take time off a more extended stay in purgatory in the next life [Figs. 2, 3].

Fig. 2 Detail of map of Ireland (1560) showing St Patrick's Purgatory

Fig. 3 St Patrick at the cave of Lough Derg

Protestant objections to an intermediate state between heaven and hell were based not so much on objections to the supernatural but to *superstition*, the idea that good works and penitential practices could contribute to salvation. As students at Wittenberg, Luther's own university, both Hamlet and Horatio are no strangers to this fear of visitations from the otherworld, but the difficulty was in establishing where the supernatural ended and superstition began. As Greenblatt points out, ghosts – and hence the whole prehistory of the Gothic – only made sense if purgatory existed, a bourne from which travellers in an afterlife could return.[32] Much robust commentary and tortured exegesis, most notably in Hobbes's *Leviathan* (1651), was devoted to those passages in the Old Testament where spirits appear, and particularly to the episode in the Book of Samuel recounting the witch of Endor's summoning up of the ghost of Samuel before a frightened Saul.[33] For Puritan divines, such apparitions bordered on Romish heresy, as is evident in the title of the Calvinist preacher, Daniel Brevint's, pamphlet of 1679, *Saul and Samuel of Endor, or the New Waies of Salvation and Service, which usually Tem[p]t Men to Rome, and Detain them there, Truly Represented and Refuted*.[34]

It was on the issue of superstition that the rebarbative culture of Gaelic Ireland parted company from the more refined Celticism of the Scottish Highlands, at least as it was filtered through the attenuated spirituality of Macpherson's Ossian and its notable precursor, William Collins's 'An Ode on the Popular Superstitions of the Highlands' (1749-50). Ghosts and visitors from the otherworld recur throughout Ossian, but they are of a spiritual rather than a superstitious provenance, and Macpherson and his apologists were careful to make subtle distinctions which elevated them above their more uncouth Homeric or Catholic counterparts. For one thing, they make no attempts to intervene in the affairs of the world, still less to answer to priestcraft or pious entreaties. As Macpherson himself points out, the heroes of ancient Caledonia were more self-reliant than those compromised 'races of men' memorialized by the bards, who looked to magic or any other *deus ex machina* to see them through:

> Any aid given their heroes in battle, was thought to derogate from their fame; and the bards immediately transferred the glory of the action to him who had given that aid. Had the poet [Ossian] brought down gods, as often as Homer hath done, to assist his heroes, his work had not consisted of eulogiums on men, but of hymns to superior beings.[35]

Related to this was the denigration of priests in Ossian: though decked out in pagan or druidic garb, there is little doubt they foreshadow their later disreputable successors:

> Their pretended intercourse with heaven, their magic and divination were the same ... [and] gained them a mighty reputation among the people. The esteem of the populace

soon increased into a veneration for the order; which these cunning and ambitious priests took care to improve, to such a degree, that they, in a manner, ingrossed the management of civil, as well as religious, affairs ... It is no matter of wonder, then, that Fingal and his son Ossian disliked the Druids, who were the declared enemies to their succession in the supreme magistracy.[36]

Like the invisible hand of Adam Smith's market economy, the supernatural was best served when it did not manifest itself through regular divine intervention, but operated unseen and offstage in human affairs. The removal of priestcraft was one way of refining the supernatural out of everyday existence; another was to associate it with subjectivity and 'fancy', or to place a screen of hearsay between reported sightings or soundings of the other world and the secular prose of everyday life. Thus in William Collins's 'Ode on the Popular Superstitions of the Highlands of Scotland', the ambiguous status of various supernatural solicitings is underlined throughout:

In scenes like these, which, daring to depart
From sober Truth, are still to Nature true
And call forth fresh delights to Fancy's view
The heroic muse employed her Tasso's art ...

How have I sat, where piped the pensive wind,
To hear his harp by British Fairfax strung.
Prevailing poet, whose undoubting mind
Believed the magic wonders which he sung!
Hence at each sound imagination glows;
Hence his warm lay with softest sweetness flows.[37]

As Peter Womack observes, the supernatural here is internalized as an aesthetic faculty, though, as he proceeds to point out, it is difficult then to determine why, on defusing of the ontology of occult experiences, they should still be an occasion of terror and fear.[38] Another strategy of this aestheticizing impulse is to project the macabre events back into bygone eras or onto outlying regions as understandable in their own (outmoded) time or place, but hardly compatible with the claims of reason in a more enlightened era. Hence the facility with which the new Gothic taste for the witches and Banquo's ghost in *Macbeth* was permitted by a topographical insistence on its location in the Scottish Highlands, in keeping with the primitivism of the periphery:

> Nor needs't thou blush that such false themes engage
> Thy gentle mind, of fairer stores possessed;
> For not alone they touch the village breast,
> But filled in elder time the historic page.
> There Shakespeare's self, with every garland crowned,
> In musing hour his Wayward Sisters found,
> And with their terrors dressed the magic scene.
> From them he sung, when midst his bold design,
> Before the Scot afflicted and aghast,
> The Shadowy kings of Banquo's fated line
> Through the dark cave in gleamy pageant passed.[39]

This ethnic turn in the Gothic did not itself go unchallenged, and with the comprehensive cultural integration of Scotland into the Union in the early nineteenth century, such panderings to superstition were perceived as giving too many hostages to a discredited past. Hence, in a striking exchange between two fictional travellers in her essay 'On the Supernatural in Poetry' (1823), Ann Radcliffe has one of her characters, Mr S-, defend the 'national costume' of the witches in *Macbeth* on the grounds that they were part of everyday, material life:

> I, now, have sometimes considered, that it was quite sensible to make Scotch witches on the stage, appear like Scotch women. You must recollect that in the superstition concerning witches, they lived familiarly upon the earth, mortal sorcerers, and were not always known from mere old women; consequently they must have appeared in the dress of the country where they happened to live, or they would have been more than suspected of witchcraft, which we find was not always the case.

As against this, his Whiggish interlocutor, Mr W-, makes a case for visibility of a different kind, calling for a clear distinction between the supernatural, and its earthly, superstitious embodiments:

> Who, after hearing Macbeth's thrilling question –
> > - What are these,
> So withered and so wild in their attire
> That look not like the inhabitants o' the earth,
> And yet are on't?

> who would have thought of reducing them to mere human beings, by attiring them not only like the inhabitants of the earth, but in the dress of a particular country, and making them downright Scotch-women, thus not only contradicting the very word of Macbeth, but withdrawing from these cruel agents of the passions all that strange and supernatural air which had made them so affecting to the imagination? ... I am speaking of the only real witch – the witch of the poet: and all our notions and feelings connected with terror accord with his. The wild attire, the look *not of this earth*, are essential traits of supernatural agents, working evil in the darkness of mystery.[40]

The true disturbance of the natural order here is that if manifestations of the supernatural lend themselves to the kind of topographical realism found in the modern novel, then the terrors of the Gothic may have less to do with the past than with modernity itself. The most telling infraction of reason throughout is not the existence of the supernatural *per se*, but its materiality or *visibility*, to the point of acquiring local colour in observing details of national costume or dress. As power was moving offstage, or rather backstage, in western liberal societies, its visible exercise, as Foucault argues, became less a show of strength than a sign of weakness, a breakdown in the system of internalized power relations that constituted hegemony.[41] For power to become visible – to show its hand – was to construe its subordinates as *other*, as not belonging to its own (cultural) world, and, accordingly, as supernatural beings leave the stage, their place is taken by new forces of irrationality, that represented by the visible markers of race, the monstrous and the modern subhuman. The two orders are not exclusive, for the persistence of superstition among lesser races was one of the badges of their inferiority, but even this acquires an additional sinister dimension when the threat from another world moves in from the periphery – where the witches in *Macbeth* were still safely located – and infiltrates civility itself, becoming indistinguishable from other 'normal' citizens of the world. In this case, visible markers of discrimination cease to function and racial discourse passes back into the Gothic, with its aptitude for addressing the darkness within 'that passeth show'. For Freud, this invisible enemy merges with the uncanny – 'on the one hand it means what is familiar and agreeable, and on the other, what is concealed and kept out of sight'[42] – but in what follows, I want to maintain that it is still a form of racial discourse, which is all the more insidious for operating below the threshold of the visible and epidermal schemas of difference.

4   WHITER SHADES OF PALE

> The Celt of Connemara, and other repealing
> peasantry, are white and not black; but it is not the
> colour of his skin that determines the savagery of a
> man. He is a savage who in his sullen stupidity, in
> his chronic rage and misery, cannot know the facts
> of the world when he sees them; whom suffering
> does not teach but only madden ... [who] brandishes
> his tomahawk against the laws of nature, and
> prevails therein as we can fancy and see.
>
> - Thomas Carlyle, 'On Repeal of the Union' (1848)

The difficulty with visibility as an index of racial
difference is best illustrated by the most influential proto-
racial classification of human beings in the eighteenth century
that codified by the great Swedish biologist, Linnaeus, in his
Systema Naturae (1758). Linnaeus distinguished several
categories of human being, some of them recognizable in
terms of later racial theory, which relegated some of the others
to 'fancy' or fiction:

Sapiens –1. Diurnus
  Wild Man. Four-footed, mute, hairy . . .
  American: Red, choleric, erect.
      Obstinate, content, free. *Paints* himself with
      fine red line. Regulated by habit.
  European: White, sanguine, brawny
      Gentle, acute, inventive. *Covered* with close
      vestments. *Governed* by custom.
  Asiatic. Yellow, melancholy, rigid.
      Severe, haughty, covetous. Covered with loose
      garments. *Governed* by opinions.
  African Black, phlegmatic, relaxed.
      Crafty, indolent, negligent. Women's bosom a
      matter of modesty, breasts give milk
      abundantly. *Governed* by caprice.

Monstrous

    (*a*)   *Alpine.*   Small,   active,   timid.
    Patagonian, large, indolent.
    (b)   Single-testicled,   so   less   fertile:
    Hottentots
    Rush-headed girls with narrow stomach:
    in *Europe*
    (c)   Long-headed,   head conic: *Chinese*
    Slant-headed, head compressed in front:
    Canadians

Troglodyte*s* –2. Nocturnus.[43]

The fictiveness here, however, is not confined to the more outlandish categories: rather, their inclusion points to the arbitrariness of the whole scheme. It is striking how the category of the wild man is still deployed for this was the heading under which the otherness of the Irish was classified since the early canonical text of colonial topography, Cambrensis's *Topographia Hibernia*. As Jacques le Goff demonstrates, Giraldus's broadside against the Irish coincides with the moment when purgatory was given its earthly co-ordinates in the northeast corner of Ireland, and indeed Lough Derg features in its bestiary of wonders, along with gold-toothed fish, bearded women, and other less heavenly creatures.[44] Ireland as a frontier space was also the site of borderline human beings, but, with the discovery of the New World on the other side of the Atlantic, it might have been expected that the demonization of Irish uncouthness would cease, and pass to even stranger lands.[45] In fact, as we have noted above, it acquired a new intensity, whether under the genocidal ferocity of the Elizabethan conquest or the religious wars of extermination under Cromwell. Much of the early colonial stereotyping in Giraldus's text – depictions of Irish life steeped in blood-drinking, cannibalism, or incest, or of Irish people at the mercy of unbridled lust, superstition, and endemic violence – was carried over into the discourses of race and the Gothic that emerged in the modern period, and given a new, biological underpinning.

Though skin colour is often taken as constitutive of the new conceptions of race, it was not singled out as a definitive quality until given full theoretical formulation in Kant's 1777 essay, 'Of the Different Human Races'. Kant linked colour directly to heredity, distinguishing between *races* and *varieties* on the grounds that when races reproduce, for example, white and black people, they produce half-breeds or a *blend* of each, whereas varieties, for example, blonde and brunettes, reproduce distinctive versions of each. Not least of the ironies here, in view of subsequent Aryan race theory, is that the distinctive character of race lies in the possibility of dilution, whereas the ability to maintain a pure blonde strain disqualifies the appellation of 'race'.[46] It was not just interbreeding that generated modifications of race. Kant also allowed for the crucial role of the environment – air, sun, terrain, and diet – in forming the configurations that races assumed over the course of humanity: 'it is only because of this natural propensity to take on the characteristics of any natural setting over many successive generations that the human form must now everywhere be subject to local modifications'. But there were limits to such climatic influences, for they could only affect the 'original lineal formation' of humanity, direct traces of which are only observable in the area 'with the most fortunate combination of both the cold and hot regions' namely, that 'between 31 and 52 degrees latitude in the old world'. Thus the asymmetry of transformations of race: white peoples are still subject to change – for the worse; but other races are fixed in their ways, and cannot change their fate. As the first major theorist on race (and a contemporary of Kant), Johann Friedrich Blumenbach, observed:

> we may fairly assume [whiteness] to have been the primitive colour of mankind, since ... it is very easy for that to degenerate into brown, but very much difficult for dark

> to become white, when the secretion and precipitation of this carbonaceous pigment ... has deeply struck root.[47]

In the most ambitious scheme of human taxonomy, Buffon's forty-four volume *Histoire Naturelle* (1749-1804), the capacity for degeneration due to climatic influences was amply illustrated by the deleterious impact of the New World on its inhabitants – by comparison with the allegedly more favourable civilizing climate of Europe. Not surprisingly, Buffon's admonitions drew the wrath of major American Enlightenment thinkers whose environmental optimism, by contrast, allowed for the possibility that white people could improve through virtue, industry, and the application of science. More remarkably, well-intentioned though misguided forms of opposition to slavery led some founding fathers, most notably Dr Benjamin Rush, to propose that, with advances in medical and moral science, black persons could also become white and take their place as equal citizens in a future republic. Considering blackness as the result of endemic leprosy caused by West African miasmas, heat, diet, and manners, Rush argued that it was slavery rather than skin colour that had brought out the worst vices of African Americans. The appearance of a 'white negro', Henry Moss, whose skin condition of white spots gradually spread from his fingers to the rest of his body, was greeted in the 1790s as a providential sign of a future egalitarian, white republic, but not every commentator was convinced.[48] Among them was Thomas Jefferson for whom the 'pallid, cadaverous white, untinged by red' colour of white negroes was itself an anomaly produced by disease. Jefferson's environmentalism extended to the racial constitution of Indians – 'The causes of this are to be found, not in a difference of nature, but of circumstance' – but not to Africans: 'that immovable veil of black, which covers all the emotions of the other'. In a revealing aside on the permeability not only of race but of humanity, Jefferson argued that the superiority of white over black was evident in black people's 'own judgment in favour of the white, declared by their preference of them, as uniformly as is the preference of the Oranootan for the black woman over those of his own species'.[49] As Blumenbach pointed out in 1795, such denigrating comparisons of human beings to apes are worthless for 'there is scarcely any other out of the principal varieties of mankind, of which one nation or another, and that too by careful observers, has not been compared, *so far as the face goes*, with the apes'.[50] Blumenbach's warning that even whites might fall victim to this comparison is prescient, given the simianization of the Irish in the mid-nineteenth century.

Environmentalism is often considered to be less disposed towards racism than its full-blooded biological counterpart, but in fact the two are deeply interrelated, as is clear from the perennial fears of miscegenation. While Benjamin Rush did envisage an eco-friendly change of complexion in the future, in which black people were 'cured' of their skin condition through habits of industry and hygiene, the fatal association with pathology and disease called in the meantime for segregation between the races, and a total prohibition on sexual relations between whites and blacks. It was possible for whites to be infected by the miasma of blackness by simply coming into contact with African Americans: 'A white woman in North Carolina not only acquired a dark colour, but several of the features of a Negro, by marrying and living with a black husband. A similar instance of a change in the colour and features of a woman in Buck's county in Pennsylvania had been observed and from a similar cause. In both cases, the women bore children by their black husbands'.[51] As with the degeneration of English settlers in Ireland excoriated by Spenser and later Cromwellian apologists, the claims of blood and good breeding are not sufficient to withstand the corrosive effects of cultural and sexual contact. Though in its early manifestations, a noxious strand in racial theory is already evident that, under the guise of medical and scientific anthropology, expanded the threat of otherness from obvious visible markers to more elusive forms of regression, exploiting distinctively modern phobias about disease, infection, and contamination. The Gothic as a mode of sensibility played a key role in legitimating this pathology, for, unlike the dominant strands in racial theory, it is obsessed with *invisible* adversaries, and fantasies of corruption, infiltration, and pollution from within. In its most virulent twentieth-century expression, this extension of epidermal to epidemiological schema led to Nazi pathologies of the Jewish threat to Aryan civilization and the vilification of Jews as disease carriers, parasites, or vermin ripe for extinction.[52] In its earlier Victorian form, however, religious bigotry and racial pathology intersected in the demonization of the Irish and the Celts, the simianized underclass that threatened the white, Caucasian race from within.

As Matthew Frye Jacobson argues in his ground-breaking study *Whiteness of a Different Colour*, not least of the complexities of modern racism is that the shift from environmental to biological explanations of race was motivated by an anxiety to distinguish *between* white races, not just to differentiate white from other coloured peoples.[53] Blumenbach's reference to facial characteristics above suggests that the relationship of race to biology and physical features was not restricted to pigmentation, even where visual appearance was concerned. Craniology and skull shape – and its later Victorian offshoots, phrenology and physiognomy – also became the province of the new 'scientific' racialism promoted by the Enlightenment, allowing for the possibility of further racial differentiation among whites and, indeed, other coloured peoples. It was the primacy of skull shape which led Blumenbach to devise the term 'Caucasian' for the most developed specimens of the white race, those that emanated from the intersection of

Europe and Asia in the region of Georgia. With an aesthetic certitude that would have pleased Stalin, if not Hitler, he explained:

> I have taken the name of this variety from Caucasus, both because its neighbourhood, and especially its southern slope, produces the most beautiful race of men, I mean the Georgian; and because all physiological reasons converge to this, that in that region, if anywhere, it seems we ought with the greatest probability to place the authochtones of mankind. For in the first place, that stock displays ... the most beautiful form of skull, from which, as from a mean and primeval type, the others diverge by the most easy gradations.[54]

By the 1830s, this was given a philological turn as the site where the Gothic and Teutonic stem of the primordial Indo-European language branched out into northern Europe, and while the Celts were originally included in this migration, the fusion of language, craniology, and empire gradually combined to exclude them from the privileged domain of true Caucasians. Central to this was John Pinkerton's *A Dissertation on the Origin and Progress of the Scythians or Goths* (1787), which was the first in a number of treatises to clearly separate the backward Celtic peoples from their Gothic or Saxon superiors. Just as the supernatural was elevated to the condition of the spiritual, gradually extricating itself from the superstition of the Highlands and Gaelic culture, so, under Pinkerton, Lowlands Scots were dissociated from their disreputable Celtic countrymen and provided with a new mythic ancestry deriving from the Picts. Not alone were Celtic claims to a civilization in antiquity suspect, but they were still in a savage state: 'The wild Irish are at the present day known to be some of the veriest savages in the globe; and have remained at the same want of civilization, as described by Greek and Roman authors, and by those of the middle ages':[55]

> [they had] yet not advanced even to the state of barbarism:
> and if any foreigner doubts this, he has only to step into the
> Celtic part of Wales, Ireland or Scotland, and look at them,
> for they are just what they were, incapable of industry or
> civilization even after half their blood is Gothic and remain
> as marked by the ancients, fond of lies and enemies of truth
> ... For the Celts were so inferior a people, being to the
> Scythians as a negro to a European, that, as all history
> shows, to see them was to conquer them.[56]

Much of Pinkerton's animus against Gaelic society, as we have seen, was directed at the cult of Ossian, notwithstanding the latter's sanitized and refined Celticism, and its proto-Arnoldian unionist sentiments. One might have expected that strong proponents of Britishness would have welcomed an integrationist aesthetic, on the grounds that it added a cultural union of sentiments to the political domination of the Celtic periphery, but, in fact, the tracing of a Pictian, Nordic ancestry laid the basis for the more overtly racist Teutonism of the nineteenth century. So far from sharing a common Scottishness with the Celtic Highlands, the Lowlands were on these premises a race apart, representing a purer strain of Anglo-Saxon identity than that of the English themselves. Given its most forceful expression in the writings of Thomas Carlyle, the relationship of the inferior Celts to Britishness was not one of integration but of subjugation, as befitted an innately inferior race. The primordial violence of conquest is the perennial condition of colonial rule, in keeping with the dictum of the Gothic genre that the sins of the fathers are visited upon subsequent generations. For James Anthony Froude, one of Carlyle's most ardent disciples, Oriental despotism was the only solution to the Irish problem, for 'right is forever tending to create might', and 'the superior part has a natural right to govern'. Unfortunately, this message is still lost on the Irish who, instead of taking their beating on the open battlefield, resort to the stealth and secrecy of terror to subvert their natural betters:

When resistance has been tried and failed – when the inequality has been proved beyond dispute by long and painful experience – the wisdom, and ultimately the duty of the weaker party is to accept the benefits that are offered in exchange for submission: and a nation which will not defend its liberties in the field, nor yet allow itself to be governed, but struggles to preserve the independence which it wants the spirit to uphold in arms, by insubordination and anarchy and secret crime, may bewail its wrongs in wild and weeping eloquence to the ears of mankind ... Ireland would neither resist courageously, nor would she honourable submit ... When insurrection finally failed, they betook themselves to assassinations and secret tribunals.[57]

The retreat from visibility thus becomes the marker of the Celtic race and the source of its biological proclivity for irrationality and violence. Crucially, this biological underpinning did not find expression in epidermal so much as *epidemiological* schemas, the notion that as a people mired in dirt, superstition and a subhuman lifestyle, the Celts were a source of pollution in the body politic. The prevalence of superstition and its grounding in material practices was sufficient by itself to account for the physical threat posed by Catholic emancipation to British public life. As an ultra-Protestant publication, *Bulwark*, expressed it in 1862: 'nearly every large town is now full of Irish papists, and the whole moral and social atmosphere of Britain, and her colonies, is infested with the malaria of the Vatican coming from the Emerald Isle'.[58] Writing earlier in the century, Samuel Coleridge gave this an additional ethnic/racial inflection through the association of Catholic virulence with the clannishness and communalism of the Irish national character. Comparing Jacobinism to the ghostly underworld of *Hamlet*, 'travelling *hic et ubique*', he deplores its 'passion and contagion' coming under 'the bewildering influences of Irish superstition, and the barbarism and virulence of Irish clanship ... the wolfish spirit even of priest-maddened

strongly poisonous. [handwritten marginal note]

41

savages': 'the venom of superstition inoculated into savagery, is at once contagious and incurable'.[59] In this remark, the process whereby the Gothic is transformed into the demonology of race is revealed: what begins as a sectarian or religious threat mutates into a form of contamination, a fear of contagion by a restless, insurgent culture.

5 'The Irish Disease': Class and Contamination

> The great fear that arose during the second half of
> the eighteenth century and that ... had its source in
> a moral myth about the plague was also the
> expression of a social concern, of a concrete political
> problem. Even if this fright adopted visions of the
> past, its birth was rooted very much in the present.
>
> - José B Monleon, *A Spectre is Haunting Europe*

As applied to the Celts – or rather, the debased variety
that constituted the Gael – this biological basis of race took
up where much American epidemiological writing left off,
depicting the Irish as disease-carriers, the pollutants of the
modern city. Taking issue with negative stereotypes of the
Irish as 'pot-bellied, bow-legged, and abortively featured ...
bearing barbarism on the very front', the American racial
theorist Josiah Nott explained that such specimens were a
'diseased stock', and could be brought back to health by
participating in the American quest for white supremacy.[60]
Unfortunately, this 'diseased stock' represented the mass of
Irish emigrants that swelled the ranks of the destitute in the
urban slums of Britain and the eastern US in the early and
mid-nineteenth century. Anxieties about crowds and
immigration were part of a general alarm about excessive
population and urban congestion raised by Thomas Malthus
in the early-nineteenth century, but such alarms were
intensified with the outbreak of the cholera epidemic in
1831-2 and the subsequent influx of pauperized Irish into the
ports and industrial heartlands of Britain. The commingling
of physical pollution with national degeneracy in the minds
of social reformers is well captured in the 'melancholy

forebodings' of Dr William Duncan about the condition of the Liverpool poor: 'I am persuaded that so long as the native inhabitants are exposed to the invasion of numerous hordes of uneducated Irish, spreading *physical and moral contamination* round them, it will be in vain to expect any sanitary code can cause fever to disappear from Liverpool'.[61]

Such dire warnings received their most forceful expression in Dr James Phillips Kay's influential account of the Irish in Manchester, *The Moral and Physical Conditions of the Working Classes*, published at the height of the cholera epidemic in 1832. As a doctrinaire *laissez-faire* economist as well as a senior physician, Kay was convinced that 'the natural tendency of unrestricted commerce', as a self-regulating system, should work to the benefit of every member of society, but this clearly was not happening in English cities. The reason could only lie outside the system, in 'foreign and accidental causes':

> A system, which promotes the advance of civilization and diffuses it all over the world ... cannot be inconsistent with the happiness of the great mass of the people ... The evils affecting the working classes, *so far from being the necessary results of the commercial system, furnish evidence of a disease which impairs its energies, if it does not threaten its vitality.*[62]

The Irish once more are the source of the 'foreign and accidental' infection that invades the system, which is it not without its ironies, given that under the Act of Union (1801) and the granting of Catholic Emancipation (1829), Ireland's purported status within the UK was no less secure than that of Lancashire itself. Moreover, as Frank Neal points out, if the interests of the employers were served by paying the minimum wage necessary for subsistence, then the tendency of the Irish to lower wages was also consistent with the logic of the system, rather than extraneous to it. Instead of all boats rising with the same tide, the immiseration of the Irish dragged the English working class down into the sewers and cesspools of their own fetid surroundings:

> The Irish have taught the labouring classes of this country a pernicious lesson ... Debased alike by ignorance and pauperism, they have discovered, with the savage, what is the minimum of the means of life ... and this secret has been taught the labourers of this country by the Irish. As competition and the restrictions and burdens of trade diminished the profits of capital, and consequently reduced the price of labour, the contagious example of ignorance and a barbarous disregard of forethought and economy exhibited by the Irish, spread. The colonization of savage tribes has ever been attended with effects on civilizations as fatal as those which marked the progress of the sand flood over the fertile plains of Egypt. [63]

The association of race with disease and contagion closes the gap between environmental and biological theories of race, for here environment is biology, in the sense of contagion through physical proximity and urban congestion. In its most pathological twentieth-century form, this became the distinctive biological stigma of Jews and gave rise to the programmes of racial hygiene and eugenics advocated by Nazi racial ideology. 'The discovery of the Jewish virus', Hitler told Himmler in 1942, 'is one of the greatest revolutions that have taken place in the world. The battle in which we are engaged today is of the same sort as the battle waged, during the last century, by Pasteur and Koch. How many diseases have their origin in the Jewish virus ... We shall regain our health only by eliminating the Jew'. As with the precedent of the Victorian Irish, moreover, part of the problem of the 'Jewish pest' was that it was largely invisible and worked through infiltration: hence the need for branding, the Star of David badge, and the 'hygienic prophylactic' (as Goebbels described it) of ghettos as a mode of social quarantine. The problem here was not *lack* but rather *ease* of assimilation: the facility with which Jews, through rapid social mobility and adaptation to the 'host' culture, passed themselves off as 'normal' citizens when, in the eyes of anti-Semitic detractors, they were secreting themselves like a virus within the system. As the French anti-Semite Edouard Drumont wrote: 'A Mr Cohen, who goes to synagogue, who keeps kosher is a respectable person. I don't hold anything against him. I do have it in for the Jew who is not obvious'.[64]

Metaphors of disease and contamination in relation to Jews drew on phobias of 'contagious lust' and sexual vampirism, which associated the erotic allure of the Jewish woman with prostitution, syphilis, and emasculating death.[65] In the case of the Victorian Irish, by contrast, the risk of contamination emanated, as we have seen, from the male as well as the female, and was associated with the spread of cholera, 'the Irish disease'. The origins of this are environmental, if by that is understood the filth and degradation of the living conditions of the Irish; but even these, as Thomas Carlyle pointed out, are due in turn to the inherent deficiencies of the Irish national character. For Carlyle, the virulent effects of cholera are reproduced politically by the contagious influence of Irishness itself on the mobilization and organization of the working class under Chartism:

> We have quarantines against pestilence; but there is no pestilence like that; and against it what quarantine is possible ... The time has come when the Irish population must either be improved a little, or else exterminated.[66]

The political threat presented by Irish pestilence is graphically illustrated by a caricature in *Punch*, published at the height of the Great Famine in 1848 when a considerable portion of the Irish population did indeed face extermination [Fig. 4]. This depicts the interior of an Irish cabin, in which a credulous Irish peasant kneels in rapt piety not in front of a Catholic altar, as one might expect, but before a display of superstitious totems from the African (or American) jungle, bearing the inscriptions 'Repeal' and 'Death to the Saxon'.

ALFRED THE SMALL,
DISGUISED AS A LITTLE WARBLER, VISITING THE IRISH CAMP;
BEING A GRAND HISTORICAL PARODY UPON ALF—D THE GR—AT VISITING THE DANISH DITTO;
And Intended for a Fresco in the New House of Parliament.

Fig. 4 'Alfred the Small', *Punch*, 16 September 1848

The repulsive appearance of the totems is accentuated by the Phrygian cap on one of them and a Napoleon type hat on the other, both of which tally with the crude pikes *cum* spears carried by the other ignoble savages (not to mention the particular obscenity of a starving child carrying a pistol). This is the image of a seditious Irish given equally sarcastic treatment by Thomas Carlyle:

> The candid Irish Confederation admits ... that England's
> work will be effectually stopped by this occupation of her
> back-parlour; and furthermore that they, the Irish
> Confederates mean it so – mean to stop England's work
> appointed by the so-called Destinies and Divine Providence.
> They, the Irish Confederates, and finest peasantry in the
> world, armed with pikes, will stop all that.[67]

The contrast with the figure of King Alfred (that is, the Prime Minister, Lord John Russell) who has infiltrated the camp – or 'back-parlour' – of the enemy disguised as a travelling player, could not be greater. King Alfred, in his mythic versions at any rate, was pivotal to the patrimony of the 'free-born Englishman', and particularly to the defence of those ancient liberties enjoyed by the lower orders which were subject to the subsequent incursions of the 'Norman yoke', and other arbitrary extensions of royal or state power. By the mid-nineteenth century, however, Anglo-Saxonism had converged with racial concepts of Teutonic destiny and, if there is any process of infiltration in the picture, it is rather the degenerate Irish who have insinuated themselves into the camp of their masters.

It is perhaps this (relatively) imperceptible marker of racial inferiority, associated with filth, human waste, and starvation, that accounts for Roy Foster's contention that popular representations of the Irish in Britain were not 'pronouncedly different in physiognomy from representations of English plebians' – and that, by extension, their whiteness immunized them from racism and related forms of bigotry:

> Their representation of all working class types was dark and
> brutish; all enemies, especially class enemies, tended to the
> monster ... the implication is that genteel journalism, on
> both sides of the Atlantic, saw the Irish as a threatening
> underclass rather than a colonized subrace.[68]

Foster is correct to draw attention to the blurring of the boundaries between class, religion, and colonial oppression, but it is not that the Irish are elevated in the process: rather, it is the English working class who are brutalized through association with the Irish, as in the classic Gothic trope of 'colonization in reverse'. In times of acute class conflict or unrest, it was precisely pathologies of racial otherness that were projected onto the metropolitan working class, as in, for example, the Africanization of the East End in London as 'the jungle within'.[69] In the Unites States, the racist ideologies of the frontier were exploited to denigrate striking workers as red savages, all the more to subject them to the full rigours of state terror, as in the case of the Molly Maguires, the Irish agrarian society that surfaced in the anthracite coalfields of Pennsylvania in the 1870s.[70] That such comparisons were possible, as Susan Thorne writes, suggests 'that "race" and "class" were not yet the antithetical or even discrete axes of identity they have since become', but it does not follow from this that there was a 'symmetry between representations of poor and colonized peoples'.[71] What is overlooked here is the *temporality* of the convergence, and the process of *degeneration*: in keeping with the notion that only whites are subject to degeneration, the urban underclass are perceived as regressing to a state beneath them, precisely by virtue of the 'contamination' of the colonies coming home to roost in the imperial centre.

The reduction of racial to class domination masks the fact that it was the porousness of the divide between the Irish 'subrace' and their industrial proletarian counterparts that posed the real threat to the incorporation of the working class as self-consciously British subjects in an era of imperial expansion. Following the lead of Linda Colley, several commentators have suggested that, as the foils against which Britishness defined itself acquired a racial dimension, they were located in the farthest outreaches of the empire, as in the draconian government responses to the Sepoy Mutiny in India in 1857, or the massacres ordered by Governor Eyre following the Morant Bay rebellion in Jamaica in 1866. According to

Catherine Hall, such racial identifications located the others of empire to the remote outposts of Caribbean and India, as if somehow the domestic delinquency of the Irish made them less estranged from the British public sphere:

> Their lordships discussed the parlous state of Ireland the same day as that of Jamaica and [Lord] Grey argued that there was 'something amiss which requires to be remedied'... Jamaica occupied a different place in their political imaginations, however, for a black majority meant a different political landscape. No one ever suggested that the white male labouring population of Ireland should be excluded from the extension of the franchise in 1867, for on the imperial scale Celts were always part of the brotherhood of Britain, albeit in a racialized and unequal position. There were 'certain peculiarities of national character' which needed to be taken into account when deciding what to do with the Irish. But such peculiarities did not legitimate disenfranchisement.[72]

But it is, in fact, through Gothic appropriations of racial theory – emphasizing disease, invisibility, and infiltration – that the Irish brought imperial demonology back to the metropolitan heartlands as the enemy within. This was the period when Fenian insurgency in England was at its height, and, far from allaying hostility towards the Irish, the coincidence of the Reform agitation with major outbreaks of Fenian violence in Britain raised once again doubts as to their whiteness, as can be seen from a pamphlet published by Earl Russell in 1866, which proposed extending the vote only to those 'independent, thoughtful voters' of native stock, who could combat 'cholera, cattle pest, the Nigger Pest – white murder, by blacks – and Fenians'. This scabrous terminology – with its linking of cholera, blackness and Irish culture - recalls the invective of Thomas Carlyle, for whom even the limited concessions of the 1867 Reform Act were nothing short of Armageddon.

6 REBELLION AND SYMPATHETIC CONTAGION

> They first alarm by sedition, then provoke by riot,
> and brave at last as open rebels.
>
> - Samuel Taylor Coleridge, *The Courier*, 1814

Whether through the association of Irish republicanism with dirt and the pigsty in Victorian caricature, or the stigmatization of Fenian insurgency as 'Fenian Fever', one of the most notable shifts in racial depictions of the Irish was the transference of moral panics raised by fears of contamination and infection from *actual* disease, typhus, and cholera, to its political counterpart, radical protest and the contagion of collective violence. Metaphors of disease had long attended condemnations of revolutionary politics, featuring prominently in Edmund Burke's dire warnings about the spread of 'the Jacobin malady', or the alarm expressed about 'the French disease' by his Irish correspondent, the Rev Thomas Hussey.[73] In his *Enquiry into the Sublime and the Beautiful* (1757), Burke described the bonds of intersubjectivity between two individuals as something that transcends their ability to convey ideas, or verbal description: 'We yield to sympathy, what we refuse to description ... by the contagion of the passions, we catch a fire already kindled in another, which probably might never have been struck out by the object described'. Elsewhere in the *Enquiry*, Burke extends this analysis to the behaviour of crowds, in which the shouting and tumult is sufficient by itself to induce individuals to throw caution to the winds regarding their own self-interest and join in the affray:

> [In] the shouting of multitudes ... the sole strength of their
> sound, so amazes and confounds the imagination, that in

the staggering, and hurry of the mind, the best established tempers can scarcely forbear being borne down, and joining in the common cry, and common resolution of the crowd.[74]

As if bearing out Burke's diagnosis of collective violence, Matthew Barrington, Crown Solicitor on the Munster Circuit, was asked in 1832 about the rapidity with which agrarian insurgency spread through the countryside:

> Your testimony goes generally to the inflammable state of the community, that they are ready prepared, and want nothing but ignition? – To a great extent it is so; and the peaceable and well-intentioned people are always compelled to join. I do not mean to give such a character to the whole population of Ireland; but I take it, that if there were twenty bad men in a barony, they would set the whole county in a flame, unless they were checked.[75]

There is a certain irony, given Burke's own close family connections to Whiteboy agitation in Ireland, that such metaphors of 'contagion' and 'ignition' became almost second nature in describing the seemingly spontaneous surges of agrarian unrest in rural Ireland, without the benefit of overt political organization or identifiable leaders, still less of revolutionary programmes.[76] During the outbreak of the Rockite insurgency in Cork in the 1820s, the most sustained campaign of agrarian protest in the early nineteenth century, one prominent landholder described the attack on his property as perpetrated 'by a party of those Whiteboys who begin to infect this neighbourhood', while another military dispatch reported that 'our neighbourhood, hitherto the most peaceful in the country, is now in a disturbed state, the infection has reached us'. As Tadhg O'Sullivan comments, the escalation of insurgency worked 'to combine the rhetoric of contamination with that of outright rebellion', leading Lord Ennismore to fulminate on the measures taken to contain the miscreants (evoking disturbing echoes of the era of Edmund Spenser and the Rev Hugh Peters):

It may be observed, that the military here prevented the contagion coming into the country where they have been placed, but they have not been able to put a stop to it where it has taken root ... *short* nights and *starvation* may do much bye and bye, but they will not put down the mischief and we shall have the uncomfortable prospect of similar work again next winter.[77]

As late as 1870, disease metaphors were still being used to explain sudden outbreaks of agrarian crime in a district, as in Lord Spencer's remark to Gladstone that while the local confinement of an eruption of Ribbonism in Westmeath was 'in some respects a cheering symptom', the 'suddeness with which a quiet county may become infected was very startling'.[78] Nor were such epidemics of crime confined to the countryside. During a formal enquiry designed to prevent the infiltration of Trinity College by the United Irishmen in the months leading up to the 1798 rebellion, Lord Clare remarked that:

he should neglect an important duty if he were to suffer it [Trinity] to continue stained with the infamous imputation of disaffection and rebellion if unfounded; or permit any guilty member thereof to poison and destroy the prospects of the unaffected ... [O]vert acts of rebellion were committed within your walls under the influence of these pestilent associations ... It remains only for us to discharge a painful part of out duty in purging this society of some of its pestilent members.[79]

One such 'pestilent member' was the young Robert Emmet, whose expulsion from Trinity College immediately followed Lord Clare's inquisition. Over twenty years later, the lethal combination of mob violence with an Irish setting reached its Gothic apotheosis in Charles Maturin's *Melmoth the Wanderer* (1820), in a scene that directly recalled Emmet's rebellion of 1803. In one of the novel's many nested narratives, an extended inner story set during the Spanish Inquisition recounts how Alonzo Moncada, having befriended a heretical monk, the Parricide, escapes from the clutches of his inquisitors when a fire engulfs his prison and its surroundings. Finding refuge with a mysterious Jew, Alonzo watches from an upstairs window as a Catholic procession attempts to wend its way through the crowded streets in reparation for the fire. To his alarm, he discerns that the Parricide is one of the monks in the procession, and no sooner has he made his discovery than the delirious crowd in the streets also notice him, and proceed to tear him to pieces in an orgy of mob violence: 'One spirit now seemed to animate the whole multitude. What had been the stifled growl of a few, was now the audible yell of all – "Give him to us – we must have him" – and they tossed and roared like a thousand waves assailing a wreck'.[80] When the cavalry rode with fury belatedly to the rescue, and asked 'where was the victim?', the answer came: 'Beneath your horse's feet'. This then provides the pretext for an explanatory footnote that brings the action to bear directly on contemporary atrocities in Maturin's Ireland:

> This circumstance occurred in Ireland 1797, after the murder of the unfortunate Mr. Hamilton. The officer was answered, on inquiring what was that heap of mud at his horse's feet, – 'The man you came for.' (344)

The Rev Dr William Hamilton, one of the founders of the Royal Irish Academy, was both Rector and Resident Magistrate at Fanaid, County Donegal, and was succeeded following his assassination by the Rev Hugh Maturin, brother of the novelist. In January 1797, Hamilton's house was besieged by over 800 insurgents after he detained some local leaders of the United Irishmen, and, while he made his escape on this occasion, United Irish assailants caught up with him in March in an adjoining district, and beat him mercilessly to death.[81] But this is not the only Irish subtext to the gory scenes of mob vengeance in *Melmoth*. Watching the carnage in the streets from his window, Alonzo confesses that, in the manner of Burke's description of the crowd, he too loses his detachment as a spectator and is drawn into the scene, alternating between identification with the crowd, and its hapless victim: 'I shrieked involuntarily when the first decisive movements began among them: but when at last the human shapeless carrion was dashed against the door, I echoed the wild shouts of the multitude with a kind of savage instinct. I bounded – I clasped my hands for a moment – then I echoed the screams of the thing that seemed no longer to live, but still could scream: and I screamed aloud and wildly for life – life – and mercy!' (344-5). This in turn provides the cue for another biographical aside on Maturin's part, alluding to the killing of Lord Kilwarden, Lord Chief Justice of Ireland, by a leaderless mob during Emmet's rebellion in 1803 [Fig. 5]:

Fig. 5 Assassination of Lord Kilwarden (1803)

In the year 1803, when Emmet's insurrection broke out in Dublin – (*the fact* from which this account is drawn was related to me by an eye-witness) – Lord Kilwarden, in passing through Thomas Street, was dragged from his carriage and murdered in the most horrid manner. Pike after pike was thrust through his body. Till at last he was *nailed to a door*, and called out to his murderers to 'put him out of his pain'. At this moment, a shoemaker, who lodged in the garret of an opposite house, was drawn to the window by the terrible cries he heard. He stood at the window, gasping with horror, his wife attempting to drag him away. He saw the last blow struck – he heard the last groan uttered, as the sufferer cried, 'put me out of pain', while sixty pikes were thrusting at him. The man stood at his window as if nailed to it; and when dragged from it, became – an *idiot for life*. (345)

The inability to stand back and achieve the comparative distance of spectatorship becomes the hallmark of the individual in Ireland when faced with the pull of the crowd: 'I for a moment', confesses Alonzo, 'believed myself the object of their cruelty. The drama of terror has the irresistible power of converting its audience into its victims' (345).

Not least of the implications of this collapse of optical distance, the reversal of roles between audience – or even perpetrator – and victim, is that it raises questions over who corresponds to what role in the Gothic genre, at least as it is manifested in the radical instability of colonial narratives in Ireland. As Fiona Robertson acutely observes in relation to *Melmoth*, the juxtaposition of the fictional target of the crowd – the terrors of the Catholic Inquisition – with the actual targets of the Protestant Ascendancy outlined in the Irish historical footnotes:

> all[ies] the crowd's immediate object of resentment, the Inquisition, with the systems of government in his own country. The alliance brings the Inquisition symbolically into line with English authority over the Irish individual, an authority treacherously supported by the Ascendancy families.[82]

In keeping with the logic of Burke's inversion of the Gothic, the forces of light and reason – the Puritan bearers of righteousness – merge with the monsters of popish superstition they are persecuting. Such an alignment of the two most formidable internal threats to the rational religion of the established Church, Catholic superstition and Puritan fanaticism, did not originate with Burke or Maturin, but had a distinguished pedigree, receiving its more influential expression, perhaps, in David Hume's essay of 1741, 'Of Superstition and Enthusiasm'. For Robert Miles, this identification of the danger of Puritan fanaticism calls for a rereading of the anti-Catholic animus of the Gothic, shifting the focus to a domestic enemy, 'that of internal, Protestant, British unease'.[83] But this unease does not by any means displace the fundamental threat posed by the anti-Catholic or colonial other, as Hume himself acknowledged. While both extremes, for Hume, err on the side of unreason, Puritanism is still preferable to Popery on the grounds that 'enthusiasm, being the infirmity of bold and ambitious tempers, is naturally accompanied by a spirit of liberty; as superstition, on the contrary, renders men tame and abject, and fits them for slavery'.[84] For Burke, by contrast, it was the bigotry of Puritanism itself that induced slavery, as was all too apparent when it gave full vent to its persecuting zeal in the colonial theatre of Ireland.

It is striking that in his indictment of Puritan Gothic, and his rhetorical counter-strike against the Protestant Ascendancy, Burke sought not only to emphasize its tainted Cromwellian origins, but also to link its legacy with the ghost of Samuel that had come to haunt the Puritan imagination. Instead of following the English example and letting 'time draw his oblivious veil over the unpleasant modes by which lordships and demesnes have been acquired',[85] the ideologues of the Protestant Ascendancy in Ireland succumb to the very forms of superstition they excoriate, and engage in triumphalist commemorations that all but release the ghosts of the past from their unquiet graves:

> One would not think that decorum, to say nothing of policy, would permit them to call up, by magic charms, the grounds, reasons, and principles of those terrible confiscatory and exterminatory periods. They would not set men upon calling from the quiet sleep of death any Samuel, to ask him by what act of arbitrary monarchs ... by what fictitious tenures, invented to dispossess whole unoffending tribes and other chieftains! They would not conjure up the ghosts from the ruins of castles and churches, to tell for what ... the estates of the old Irish nobility and gentry had been confiscated. They would not wantonly call on those phantoms, to tell by what English acts of parliament, forced upon two reluctant kings, the lands of their country were put up to a mean auction in every goldsmith's shop in London; or chopped to pieces, and cut into rations, to pay the mercenary soldiery of a regicide usurper. They would not be so fond of titles under Cromwell, who, if he revenged an Irish rebellion against the sovereign authority of the parliament of England, had himself rebelled against the very parliament whose sovereignty he asserted full as much as the Irish nation, which he was sent to subdue and confiscate, could rebel against that parliament ...[86]

Burke's heightened language here has shifted into a Gothic register, as if the excess of hatred unleashed by successive waves of conquest can no longer be contained. The ghosts of the Catholic/Gaelic order indeed roam the landscape, but that is because they have been released from their vaults by recurrent Protestant terror. Burke had no illusions about what Seamus Heaney has referred to as the 'abattoir of history' and, notwithstanding his attack on the French Revolution, went so far as to argue that revolution and political convulsions were often necessary to jolt a system out of torpor and decay. But if this violence becomes perpetual, if coercion and intimidation cannot be laid to rest, and the terrors of the sublime ameliorated by the beautiful (as he put in the *Enquiry*), then we are in the territory of the Gothic. Here the sins of the fathers are visited continually on the present, and in case they are not, the descendants of the original transgressors insist on reminding the victims of the unrequited grievances, to beat them further into the clay. For Burke, to rekindle their smouldering resentments of the past in this triumphalist manner is to risk a conflagration in the present, giving rise to a different, incendiary sublime, a transport out of oneself which results in collective contagion and incessant popular insurgency

It is this troubled inheritance that also informs Maturin's conception of the Gothic. In *The Milesian Chief* (1812), the theme of usurpation is taken from *The Castle of Otranto* but transplanted onto a colonial Irish landscape, the setting for the return of the Anglo-Irish landlord, Lord Montclare, to 'reclaim' his estate from the eponymous native Milesian chief. No sooner has his daughter, the beautiful Armida, caught her first glimpse of the wild scenery than she encounters the displaced Milesian chieftain and his family:

> compelled to inhabit ruins by tracing among them the remains of ancient palaces; that like the spirit in Otranto stalks amid its ancient seat till it smells [sic] beyond it, and stands forth amid the fragments dilated and revealed, terrifying the intrusion of modern usurpers ... A thousand gloomy thoughts of Irish atrocity rushed to her mind ... What if the Milesian prince or his grandson were come to curse the usurpers of their castle by the only light their pride would permit them to view its alienated walls by?[87]

In *Melmoth*, the 'intrusion of modern usurpers' is dated from the arrival of the Melmoth family in Ireland with Cromwell, and their securing, as the old crone Biddy Brannigan informs us, 'a grant of lands, the confiscated property of an Irish family attached to the royal cause' (64). The opening scenes of the novel are set in a gaunt, dilapidated demesne on a windswept Wicklow landscape, and relate how a mysterious member of the original colonizing family, the Traveller Melmoth, is doomed to wander the earth, and is still stalking the family estate as if in atonement for the original sin of its acquisition. As several commentators have pointed out, though an Anglican clergyman of Calvinist convictions (as he described himself), Maturin's work is imbued with the taint of irredeemable guilt and almost preternatural fears of the terrors conjured up – or unleashed – by the Puritan imagination. In keeping the paradigm-shift in the Gothic genre effected by Burke, the ineluctable political bind of the 'colonial garrison' (as Burke called it) in Ireland was that, notwithstanding the much vaunted civility of the established Church, it was unable to throw off the sectarian shackles of its Cromwellian forbears, and hence never ceased to remind the dispossessed of the ill-gotten origins of Protestant Ascendancy. While Protestant liberty basked in the reflected glory of the 1688 revolution in Britain, the arbitrary oppression of the Penal Laws, and the persecution of Catholics during the Whiteboy unrest in the 1760s and across Ireland as a whole in the 1790s, attested to the persistence of the manic political strain in Protestant Gothic exemplified by the Rev Hugh Peters. Cowed though they were into subjection, the Catholic population never acceded through consensus, and the abiding fear of the 'colonial garrison' was that underneath expressions of loyalty and outward conformity lay a barely concealed hatred and unrequited rage for justice. 'Superstition', wrote Hume, 'steals in gradually and insensibly; renders men tame and submissive; is acceptable to the magistrate and inoffensive to the people; till at last the priest, having firmly established his authority, becomes the tyrant and disturber of human society ... How smoothly did the Romish church advance in her acquisition of power'.[88] By the nineteenth century, this capacity for sly sedition has passed from the priest to an even greater 'disturber of human society', the conspiratorial, revolutionary underground of the clannish Celts.

7 'FENIAN FEVER': CELTS AND CONSPIRACY

> What brotherhood ought you to have with the
> 'United Irishmen' party, who pride themselves on
> their hatred to your nation, and recommend
> schemes of murder which a North American Indian
> ... would account horrible.
>
> - Charles Kingsley, 'Letter to the Chartists' (1848)

The framing story in Maturin's novel, recounting the
troubled, Cromwellian origins of the Melmoth family in
Ireland is related by a withered old hag, Biddy Brannigan,
whose demeanour of sly servility on her introduction to the
young John Melmoth becomes a staple in descriptions of the
Irish peasantry:

> She came, and, on her introduction to Melmoth, it was
> curious to observe the mingled look of servility and
> command, the result of the habits of her life, which was
> alternatively one of abject mendacity, and of arrogant but of
> clever imposture. When she first appeared, she stood in the
> door, awed and curtseying in the presence, and muttering
> sounds which, possibly intended for blessings, had, from
> the harsh tone and witch-like look of the speaker, every
> appearance of malediction. (62)

The malediction here points to another aspect of disease
that, like contagion, adds a racial dimension to what might
otherwise be seen as class domination or inequality. This has
to do with 'imposture', duplicity, and invisibility – the fear
that the threat presented by the other is all the more
insidious when it is not conspicuous or easily identified. As
in the case of Jews passing for respectable members of the
bourgeoisie, the Irish, by dint of their (not always evident)
whiteness, could circulate among the English working class
while contaminating it to the core. Though imbued with

biological associations, this contamination was of an economic kind as the tendency of destitute Irish labourers to drive down wages was perceived as reducing the condition of the advanced working class to abject Irish living standards – the very standards British culture prided itself on transcending. In this, the Irish were cast in the role of reactionary scab labour against the English working class but, as Frederick Engels was quick to note, their actual political effect was revolutionary, insofar as it drove a wedge between the working class and the integrative, consensual ideology of Englishness – or its imperial cognate, Britishness. The ideological drive for order and stability sought to cut the respectable working class off from the lumpen or pauperized underclass, thus creating a divide between the honest and upright labouring poor, and the ragged hordes who were seen as infesting the ghettoes and back-lanes of the city. Central to this was an investment in patriotism, which ensured that the mark of the advanced working class was not their militant consciousness but their Britishness – and superiority to lesser breeds.[89] 'In this manner', writes Margot Finn, 'the national idiom of Victorian radicalism undercut the language of class, encouraging collaboration between Liberals and Chartists by underscoring their shared ancestry in a radical tradition that predated industrial capitalism'.[90]

For Marx and Engels, it was the forging of a common bond between masters and men, nurtured through habits of imperial and racial superiority, which posed the main obstacle to the revolutionary potential of the advanced working class:

> The ordinary English worker hates the Irish worker as a competitor who causes a drop in wages and the standard of life. He feels national and religious antipathy towards him. He regards him in almost the same way as the poor whites of the Southern States of North America regarded black slaves.

But Marx goes beyond this to say that it is not just a matter of living standards: the political and economic identification with Britishness militates against the radicalization of the working class, in marked contrast with the 'embittered' and incendiary discontent of the Irish poor:

> The English have all the material prerequisites for the social revolution. What they lack is a spirit for generalization and revolutionary fervour ... The revolutionary fervour of the Celtic worker does not fit in with the slow temperament of the Anglo-Saxon worker; on the contrary, in all the large industrial centres of England there is a profound antagonism between the Irish proletarian and the English proletarian.[91]

For Engels, the role of the Irish as a catalyst in the English labour movement took on a related racial cast as when, contesting Carlyle's 'prejudice in favour of the Teutonic character', he outlines the characteristic traits of the Irish temperament: 'With the Irish, feeling and passion predominate: reason must bow before them. Their sensuous, excitable nature prevents reflection and quiet persevering activity from reaching development'.[92] Engels appears to agree with Carlyle's racial profile, except he places a different valuation on it. Instead of expressing alarm over the racial intermixing of Anglo-Saxon and Celt, moreover, he positively advocates such an infusion, and looks forward 'to the abundance of hot Irish blood that flows in the veins of the English working class' to precipitate them out of their cautious British moderation (239). Not surprisingly, given the references to 'blood' and 'veins', the diagnosis of the revolutionary potential of alliances between the Irish and English working classes also looks to the language of disease:

> Another influence of great moment in forming the character of the English workers is the Irish immigration already referred to. On the one hand it has, as we have seen, degraded the English workers, removed them from

civilization, and aggravated the hardship of their lot; but, on the other hand, it has thereby deepened the chasm between workers and bourgeoisie, and hastened the approaching crisis. For the course of the social disease from which England is suffering is the same as the course of a physical disease; it develops according to certain laws, has its own crises, the last and most violent of which determines the fate of the patient. And, as the English nation cannot succumb under the present crisis, but must go forth from it, born again, rejuvenated, we can but rejoice over everything which accelerates the course of the disease. And to this the Irish immigration further contributes by reason of the passionate, mercurial temperament, which it imports into England and into the English working class. (153)

Damning the Irish with faint praise indeed, it is difficult not to suspect here that the recourse to racial terminology derives from the blurred boundaries between disease as both *physical* and *political* contagion, and to Carlylean notions of the crowd as a political force operating primarily at a somatic, pre-linguistic level, and hence prone to disease and contagion.[93] There is a certain irony in that one of the distinctive *historical* products which the Irish did bring with them to Britain, a capacity for collective organization and social solidarity derived from the communalism of the Irish land system, was itself attributed to race and national character, and removed from history. This is nowhere more evident than in the contrast drawn by Victorian theorists between the alleged traits of the Teutonic and Celtic races, according to which the Teutonic – or, more ominously, Aryan – race was seen as the exemplar of manly individualism, and its religious offshoot, Protestantism, while the Celts preferred to hunt in packs (hunting being the operative metaphor for the savage state) and to bow to superstition and ritual. In the eyes of Dr Isaac Taylor, as formulated in his *Origin of the Aryans* (1889), this contrast came complete with craniological measurements, and impeccable Low Church, Unionist pedigrees for the master race:

> Now that Christianity has spread over Europe, it is divided into two opposed camps – the Catholic and the Protestant, the Church of Authority and the Church of Reason, the line of decision coinciding very closely with the line which separates the two great races of Aryan speech. The dolichocephalic Teutonic race is Protestant; the brachycephalic Celto-Slavic race is either Roman Catholic or Greek Orthodox. In the first, individualism, wilfulness, self-reliance, independence, are strongly developed; the second is submissive to authority and conservative in instincts ... The Lowland Scotch, who are more purely Teutonic than the English, have given the freest development of Protestantism. Those Scotch clans who have clung to the old faith have the smallest admixture of Teutonic blood. Ulster, the most Teutonic province in Ireland, is the most firmly Protestant ... In Galway and Kerry it has no footing.

But in case he has given the impression that religion has entirely gone to his head, he adds a rider: 'It is not to be supposed, however, that religious belief is a function of the shape of the skull, but that the shape of the skull is one of the surest indications of race'.[94]

In bringing the spurious precision of evolutionary theory to bear on the case against Home Rule, the most telling aside concerns the exclusion of the clannish Highlanders and their unfortunate Irish counterparts in Galway and Kerry from the 'Church' of reason. If the Teutonic peoples were distinguished – in their own eyes, at any rate – by individualism, self-reliance, and their leadership qualities, those of a Celtic temperament were sociable to a fault in that by clinging to others; they were unduly impressionable and subject to a slave mentality: 'The Lowlander, *self-relying*', wrote John Hill Burton, in his *History of Scotland* (1853), 'gave as little effect as he could to the *feudal constraints that bound him to a leader*. The Highlander could not do without one. He naturally clung to anyone whom nature placed in a position to command him'. But as JM Robertson points out in his formidable contemporary critique of Victorian racism, no sooner has Burton passed this verdict on their submissiveness than 'he unfalteringly cites it as a fresh crime against the Celts that they would *not* obey their leaders'. As Burton laments: 'They had a system of discipline of their own, very lax and precarious, and they would work in no other. They would follow no leaders and obey no commander but those whom the accident of birth had set over them; and the highest military skill was lost in any attempt to control them'. As Robertson proceeds to demonstrate, Burton does not let the facts get in the way of his argument:

> At one place Burton takes up for a moment the suggestion, supported by historical data which he does not pretend to dispose of, that under their own institutions, in a propitious territory, the Celts could get on well enough; and this is how he gets rid of it:- 'All doctrines are entitled to a hearing (!); but this one leads to conclusions so unharmonious to all established belief in the blessed influences of peace and industry, that it will require support from a more consolidated supply of facts, than theorists about the Irish and the Highlanders are generally cogent with' – this with some of the facts lying in his own footnotes.

The Celts, it would seem, were not the only ones to react against the despotism of fact; the problem, however, was that they also reacted against the despotism of empire and brought this rebellious spirit into the industrial heartlands of England itself. As Feargus O'Connor, the Chartist leader, proposed of the mechanics of power, exploiting the reputation of the fighting Celts that had been enlisted in the ranks of the imperial army:

> [the English working class] should be the main-spring of the watch; - the Irish – a war-like people, and the Scotch – a war-like people, should be the outer works; and when they (the main-spring) moved, with their moral force, the

Paddies and the Scots would begin to move with something else (deafening cheers). Paddy had been for a long time more disciplined than they were, and knew better how to deal with the parsons and the army; the Scotch, who fought for the great Covenant before, would fight for their rights now.[95]

It was not the anti-social nature of the Celt but the fact that they were all *too social* that posed the problem. Hence the persistent anxiety over the intense social solidarity of the Irish and their clear organizational and leadership skills, especially when it came to emergent trade-union consciousness, mass demonstrations or militant politics. Dangerous as Jacobinism was in the eyes of Coleridge, it took on a new deadly form in Ireland through:

> the delusive and pernicious sublimation of local predilection and clannish pride, into a sentiment and principle of nationality. This is sufficiently observable in North Britain, and among the lower ranks of the Welsh; but nowhere is it so generally diffused, nor produces so delusive an influence, as in Ireland. Those feelings which in their proper place, form the strength and glory of our nature, be so transferred as to become of all others most imperious. Take, as illustration, the reverence of supernatural power transferred to the senses, and trace its effects on lewd and sanguinary abominations ...

The corrupting influence of superstition is complemented by the secrecy and slavish obedience to the Catholic Church, but with an additional ethnic component provided by the opacity of the Irish language. A second example of the degeneration of a good human quality:

> is presented to us in the social instinct ... perverted to conspiracy and a blind submission to its remorseless leaders, and fanatical by-laws ... The impracticality of subduing the conspiracy by law, not merely from its unprecedented extent, and the multitude, ignorance, and ferocity of the Oathsman ... but likewise from the facilities of concealment afforded by the Erse language.[96]

Following the logic of Coleridge's own – and Engels' – disease metaphor, a process of collective contagion was indeed activated by the Irish, deriving from the clandestine social and political networks they brought with them to Britain, America, and Australia. That this was perceived as contamination of the individualism of the free-born Englishman is clear from a deposition to the *Royal Commission on the Condition of the Poorer Classes* in 1836: '[The Irish] are more prone to take part in trades unions, combinations and secret societies than the English; [moreover] they are talkers and ringleaders on all occasions'. The difficulty here was not restricted to the more obvious 'ringleaders' such as John Doherty, the founder of the first national-based trade union, or to radical Chartists leaders such as O'Connor, and his countrymen James Bronterre O'Brien and John Cleave. These at least were known to the public: the Gothic element is imparted through the persistent alarms over the Celtic aptitude for conspiracy and violence, aided and abetted by the Jesuit cunning of the Catholic Church. As John Plotz suggests, for all their potential for violence, the openness of mass politics and disciplined street demonstrations were deemed preferable by the authorities to secret societies,[97] but the paradox in the case of the Irish (or even Irish leadership) was that, insofar as they lent themselves to control and discipline, these were seen as a front for ulterior, conspiratorial designs.[98] 'The present moment is a ramification of the Irish conspiracy', *The Times* warned on 10 April 1848, the day of the monster Chartist meeting on Kennington Common: 'The Repealers wish to make as great a hell of this island as they have made of their own'. As mass unrest intensified following outbreaks of revolution in Ireland and the continent, the authorities targeted, as at Manchester, 'all the leading agitators who have for some time past *infested* this City and the neighbouring towns', led by the likes (as *Punch* expressed it) of 'MOONEY, ROONEY, HOOLAN, DOOLAN'.[99]

It was not until the outbreak of 'Fenian Fever' in the 1860s that fears of Irish infection of the working class and middle-class civility gave way to a fully fledged political Gothic, visualized above all in the pages of *Punch* and like-minded periodicals. Though James Stephens, the founder of the Irish Republican Brotherhood, liked to claim that the sophisticated organizational networks of the new Fenian movement had thrown off its more shadowy agrarian ancestors, such as the Ribbonmen, this was not the perception in Britain and the US. The moral panic induced by the Molly Maguires in the 1870s, already alluded to above, indicated that fears about the resurrection of the Irish political undead were well founded. In this convergence between race, agrarian societies, and political conspiracy, there are also traces of the earlier Irish transatlantic menace which, under the pretext of the infiltration of the United Irish *émigrés* by the Jacobin Illuminati, led to the passing of the Alien and Sedition Act in 1797, and the emergence of the paranoid style in American politics.[100] As with the Illuminati, the Molly Maguires were characterized by their penchant for hermetic ritual, mystery, and murder. According to Franklin B Gowan, the most prominent representative of the mining interests, who also doubled up as District Attorney for the region:

> The coal regions are infested by a most desperate class of men, banded together for the worst purposes – called, by some, the Buckshots, by others, the Molly Maguires ... As far as we can learn, the society is of foreign birth, a noxious weed which has been transplanted from its native soil – that of Ireland – to the United States, some time within the past twenty years. It lived and prospered in the old country considerably earlier. *Its supporters there were known as Ribbonmen, the Whiteboys, and sometimes as Molly Maguires, but their modes of procedure were the same as now pursued in the coal regions* ... Wherever anthracite is employed is also felt

the vice-like grip of *this midnight, murderous minded fraternity* ... wherever hard coal is used for fuel, there the Molly Maguire leaves his slimy trail and wields with deadly effect his two powerful levers – secrecy, combination ... What we want, and everybody wants, is to get within this apparently impenetrable ring; turn to the light the hidden side of this dark and cruel body, to probe to its core this festering sore upon the body politic, which is gradually gnawing into the vitals and sapping the life of the community.[101]

If the original Gothic was driven, in part, by Whig, Protestant misgivings about the residues of Catholic influence, this acquired an added racial and political intensity through associations of clandestine Jesuit cunning with the political contagion of terror and subversion. Central to this were an anxiety over the inscrutability of the enemy and the identification of 'impenetrable' Masonic/Catholic-style rituals as the means whereby normal whiteness passed over into the underworld of darkness. On the cover of a sectarian polemic entitled *The Unknown Power behind the Irish Nationalist Party: Its Present Work and Criminal History* (1908), a Gothic assassin is depicted, writing the annals of Irish 'Past History', 'Blood', 'Murder', etc., with a bloodstained hand, which drips onto skulls and bones below [Fig. 6]. The publication, edited by the ultra-Unionist Right Hon Lord Ashtown, is dedicated to establishing sinister conspiratorial links between secret societies such as the Whiteboys, the Defenders, the Ribbonmen and Molly Maguires, revolutionary movements such as the United Irishmen and the Fenian Clan na Gael organization, and, last but not least, 'respectable' Irish organizations such as the Ancient Order of Hibernians, the United Irish League, and the Irish Nationalist party.

Fig. 6 'The Unknown Power'

An illustration of 'A Secret Meeting of Ribbonmen', featuring a complicit female servant, raised glasses, shillelaghs, and oathtaking [Fig. 7], is followed a few pages later by a depiction of another elaborate ritual, the induction of the informer McKenna (alias the detective McParlan) into the AOH/Molly Maguires, under the far from spiritual guidance of a crucifix on the wall [Fig. 8].

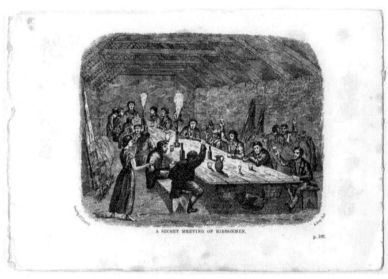

Fig. 7 'A secret meeting of Ribbonmen'

Fig. 8 'McKenna Received into the Ancient Order of Hibernians'

The key to the totalizing sweep of this conspiracy is the emphasis on secrecy and opacity, the fact that having undergone these arcane rituals, ordinary white folk have become agents of terror but are still indistinguishable from those around them. In Sir Arthur Conan Doyle's late Sherlock Holmes mystery, *The Valley of Fear* (1914), the worldwide threat posed by Irish terror is exposed through linking the Molly Maguires with the scheming genius of the master of invisibility and 'self-effacement', Professor Moriarty.[102] The story is one of deceit, imposture, and multiple identities as a Pinkerton agent assumes the guise of an AOH (called the 'Eminent Order of Freeman' in the story) man on the run, one John McMurdo from County Monaghan, to infiltrate the Molly Maguires (renamed the 'Scowrers' in the story). McMurdo's appearance and demeanour mark him as both Irish and ordinary, yet raise questions at the outset that all is not immediately apparent to the eye:

> It is easy to see that he is of a sociable and possibly simple disposition, anxious to be friendly to all men. Anyone could pick him at once as gregarious in his habits and communicative in his nature, with a quick wit and a ready smile. And yet the man who studied him more might discern a certain firmness of jaw and grim tightness about the lips which would warn him there were depths beyond, and that this pleasant, brown-haired young Irishman might conceivably leave his mark for good or evil upon any society to which he was introduced. (86)

This becomes a central motif of the story, and is extended to members of the organization itself, whose appearances belie the twisted personalities underneath:

> Among the older men there were many whose features showed the tigerish, lawless souls within, but looking at the rank and file it was difficult to believe that these eager and open-faced young fellows were in truth a very dangerous gang of murderers, whose minds suffered such complete

> moral perversion that they took a horrible pride in their
> proficiency at their business, and looked with deepest
> respect at the man who had the reputation of making what
> they called a 'clean job'. (114)

It is in the faces of the leaders of the society, and particularly their head, Boss McGinty, that the traces of racial degeneration and the physiognomy of evil betray their presence. 'They were outwardly respectable citizens, well clad and cleanly: but a judge of faces would have read little hope ... in those hard mouths and remorseless eyes' (162). As Catherine Wynne points out in her study of the colonial Conan Doyle, leading racial theorists were not slow to account for the psychological instability of the political rebel or revolutionary in terms of degeneration. According to Max Nordau:

> In view of Lombroso's researches, it can hardly be doubted
> that the writings and acts of revolutionists and anarchists
> are also attributable to degeneracy. The degenerate is
> incapable of adapting himself to existing circumstances.
> This incapacity, indeed, is an indication of morbid variation
> in every species, and probably a primary cause of their
> sudden extinction. He therefore rebels against conditions
> and views of things which he necessarily feels to be painful,
> chiefly because they impose on him the duty of self-control,
> of which he is incapable on account of his organic weakness
> of will.[103]

McGinty comes across almost as a laboratory specimen of the degenerate Celtic Jeykll and Hyde, conducting his meetings with a 'purple stole round his neck; so that he seemed to be a priest presiding over some diabolical ritual':

> All else in the man – his noble proportions, his fine features,
> and his frank bearing – fitted in with that jovial, man-to-
> man manner which he affected. Here, one would say, is a
> bluff, honest fellow, whose heart would be sound however
> rude his outspoken words might seem. It was only when
> those dead, dark eyes, deep and remorseless, were turned

on a man that he shrank within himself, feeling that he was face to face with an infinite possibility of latent evil, with a strength and courage and cunning behind it which made it a thousand times more deadly (103).

In keeping with the earlier fusion of savagery and sentimentality in the warrior cult of Ossian, members of the organization are much given to music, particularly when there is whiskey in the offing. 'Here were men to whom murder was familiar ... and yet the tender and pathetic in music could move them to tears. McMurdo has a fine tenor voice, and if he had failed to gain the good will of the lodge before, it could no longer have been withheld after he thrilled them with "I'm Sitting on the Stile, Mary", and "On the Banks of the Allan Water" ' (121). Though the acerbic Holmes espouses the principles of 'pure reason' (11) in dealing with such forces of darkness, the story shows in fact that, in Gothic fashion, the enemy can only be defeated by going over to the other side, outdoing him in dissembling and – though this is not so readily admitted – his capacity for terror. As Catherine Wynne summarizes it, 'Holmes internalizes criminality in order to destroy it' – the difficulty here being not only that the other has infiltrated civil society, but that civil society itself has to arm itself with the weapons of the enemy to defeat it.[104]

It is in this sense that the Gothic picks up where the visibility of race leaves off, the language of contagion extending the racial typologies of 'extreme cases' to the entire membership of a group. The Gothic's preoccupation with deceit and subterfuge were originally related to doubts over religious conversion, the ease with which a member of an ostracized group could gain admission to the dominant culture by conforming to certain external or legal protocols. In eighteenth-century Ireland, the fact that such apostasy was necessary to own landed property, enter the professions, or indeed to participate in public life, reinforced Protestant suspicions of Catholic duplicity, of outward acquiescence but inner disloyalty. More than perhaps any other public figure in this period, Edmund Burke ran the gauntlet of profound distrust and suspicion, his High Church Protestantism masking in the eyes of his detractors a crypto-Catholicism, nurtured through family affiliations with Jacobites and Whiteboys, and an alleged secret Jesuit education at St Omer in France. The granting of Catholic Emancipation was tantamount to admitting this kind of duplicity into the public sphere, so that constitutional campaigns for Repeal or political reforms in general were perceived as stalking horses for subversion and political terrorism. 'I belong to a society that I know only as an innocent one', protests Mc Murdo of his membership of the Eminent Order of Freeman in *The Valley of Fear*: 'You'll find it through the length and breadth of the States; but always as an innocent one. Now, when I am counting upon joining it here, you tell me that it is the same as a murder society called the Scowrers' (97). In this world of blurred boundaries where margins become the centre, no one was above suspicion. Setting out for Pennsylvania, McMurdo might have arrived, for all practical purposes, in Transylvania.

8 THE VAMPIRE STRIKES BACK

> In 1848, at Fox Farm in the state of New York, the first séances of modern spiritualism were conducted. The same year, across the Atlantic, Marx and Engels published the *Communist Manifesto*, with the now famous introductory sentence, 'A Spectre is haunting Europe – the spectre of Communism'. The language of esotericism connects two apparently unrelated events ... As with the Gothic production, the recall of primitiveness, of 'backwardness', announced the form of things to come.
>
> - José B Monleon, *A Spectre is Haunting Europe*

Nothing illustrates colonial misgivings over the admission of the Irish into the public sphere, and the ambiguous nature of their integration into British society, than an incident recounted by Bram Stoker in his *Personal Reminiscences of Henry Irving*. During a holiday on the Isle of Wight, Stoker fell into an argument with Irving on the question of Home Rule, the actor's impatience with the issue becoming abundantly clear when he inquired whether 'the hideous strife of politics' had a place at all in the tranquility of the English countryside. At that point, a policeman on foot-patrol passed by, providing Irving with an opportunity to confirm his view:

> 'Here comes the Voice of England. Just listen to it and learn ... Tell me, officer, what is your opinion as to this trouble in Ireland?'
>
> The answer came at once, stern and full of pent up feeling, and in an accent there was no possibility of mistaking:
>
> 'Ah, begob, it's all the fault iv the dirty Gover'mint!' His brogue might have been cut with a hatchet. From his later

conversation – for of course after that little utterance, Irving led him on … I came to the conclusion that Home Rule was of little consequence to that guardian of the law; he was an out and out Fenian.[105]

As Joseph Valente points out in his *Dracula's Crypt: Bram Stoker, Irishness and the Question of Blood*, such an example of incomplete, even contradictory, incorporation into British culture may well have applied to Stoker himself, encumbered by his brogue and Irishness even as he made his way up the social ladder in Irving's distinguished social milieu.[106] For Stoker – and for late Victorian culture – race was essentially a matter of *blood*, and the ease with which Count Dracula enters the mainstream of British society plays on anxieties about its relationship to disease, heredity, and cultural intermixing. The Count's uncertainty over his accent – 'True, I know the grammar and the words, but yet I know not how to speak them' – and his determination to slip unnoticed into English society 'so that no man stops if he see me, or pause in his speaking if he hear my words, to say, "Ha, ha! A stranger!"',[107] links him initially to Irishness, and it is in keeping with this, as noted by Seamus Deane, that he arrives appropriately in a 'coffin ship' of the kind that transported thousands of disease-ridden, starving Irish during the Famine. However, this far from exhausts the manifold Irish subtexts in *Dracula*, and it is when Deane proceeds to associate the decadent Count also with the parasitic, absentee landlord class that Valente identifies not just a case of transfusion but of confusion:

> [A] contradiction … obtains, however, between Dracula's symbolic connection with the Anglo-Irish Ascendancy and with its political nemesis, the racially mixed but Gaelic-identified Fenian movement … A recent piece of scholarly confusion attests as much. Having identified Dracula as an absentee Anglo-Irish landlord, Seamus Deane proceeds to observe, ignoring the implicit contradiction, that the count's conveyance to England is literally a 'coffin ship', the name given to dangerous and disease-ridden vessels carrying the

poorest Irish emigrés to foreign shores and, needless to say, enjoying no Ascendancy patronage whatsoever.

The contradiction in this, according to Valente, is readily apparent: 'One was either an agent of colonialism – *a la* Dracula the Ascendancy landlord ... or one was the object of colonialism – *a la* Dracula the Irish urban lumpen' – but one cannot be both at the same time.[108] Yet the central issue in the analysis of nineteenth-century Ireland was precisely the links between the two, insofar as it was the landlord class in Ireland that was responsible for the coffin ships, and offloading the remnants of the pauperized Irish peasantry onto the advanced working class of the metropolitan centre. 'Unless my senses deceive me', reflects Jonathan Harker in *Dracula*, 'the old centuries had, and have, powers of their own which mere 'modernity' cannot kill'.[109] For Matthew Arnold, the conjunction of the imaginative (but, of course, subordinate) Celt with the rational, utilitarian Saxon could only lead to the regeneration of the Union, but for Stoker, any claim to *equality* in such a relationship entailed a radically different political trajectory:

> And now, amongst these others, comes forth this old-world people – seeming half-barbarous amid an age of luxury, but with strength and pride intact, and claims its position, as, at least, their equal.[110]

In the original Gothic, the residual threats posed by Catholicism and a feudal, aristocratic order were fused in the one social order, but the paradox of colonial Ireland was that while both existed in the same polity, they were on the opposite sides of the social spectrum. It was the Protestant interest – indeed, in the popular imagination, the descendants of Cromwellian planters – who were the parasitic landlords, while the collective contagion of the urban crowd, in its militant, subversive forms, had passed into the hands of the subaltern Catholic classes.

To the degree that racial theory drew on the demonology of the Gothic, it extended its acts of exclusion beyond the visible markers of skin colour to a more elusive social underworld, having to do with secret societies, collective violence, class pollution, or other sources of degeneration. However, this incorporation of the Gothic carried its own ideological risks, for, as a genre residing in the protean nature of language and symbolic form, it did not lend itself to absolute mastery or control. While biology was held to be fixed in nature, literary genres were far from immutable and, by their versatility, produced the kind of transgressions in the 'natural order' of race that the supernatural effected in the natural world of the Gothic. Through acts of appropriation and rhetorical counter-strikes, the conventional Gothic could, like Dracula, jump ship in Ireland, and come back to haunt the modernizing Protestant mentality that devised it in the first place. Thus we find, at one level, the conventional Gothic association of the forces of darkness with the insurgency of the Catholic underworld in a dramatic illustration of a precursor of Captain Moonlight in the British periodical, *The Tomahawk*, one of the main rivals to *Punch*. Accompanied by the captions 'Agrarian murder in Ireland has increased tenfold during the last half year', and 'It is said that a dead vampire can be restored to life by the moonbeams', we see a Chatterton-like depiction of a prostrate Irish peasant, a member of an agrarian secret society, rising from the grave under the influence of a moonbeam spelling out the word, in ghostly capitals, 'IMPUNITY' [Fig. 9].[111]

Fig. 9 'The Irish Vampire', *The Tomahawk*, 7 August 1869

If Captain Moonlight is acting with impunity, it is due to the lack of resolve in enforcing law and order; if, on the other hand, the colonial government is placed in the position of answering force with greater force, no veil of legitimacy can hide the fact that it too is engaged in terror, which keeps alive the memory of its own primordial acts of confiscation and violence.

By the 1880s, in the pages of *Punch*, the nocturnal leadership of Captain Moonlight and his hillside men had passed over into parliamentary politics itself, in the personage of Charles Stewart Parnell, who is portrayed as a vampire preying on the innocent (though voluptuous) body of Hibernia, with her broken harp [Fig. 10].[112] As in the case of the Molly Maguires and the Ancient Order of Hibernians, Irish constitutional politics merges with political insurgency in a form of racial paranoia that construes violence itself as a product of the Irish national character.

Fig. 10 'The Irish Vampire', *Punch*, 24 October 1885

But there is an additional political irony to Parnell's credentials as a vampire for, as several critics have recently argued, not least of the ambiguities surrounding him was that as a Protestant landlord himself, he too is aligned with the tradition of bloodsucking landlords who gained their ascendancy under the grim catalogue of seventeenth-century conquests.[113] The very rhetorical force of *Punch's* image draws upon – or releases – a semantic field of counter-associations that stand as an indictment of colonial rule in Ireland. The ease with which colonial Gothic could be turned against itself is clear from a cartoon which followed in the nationalist *Freeman's Journal* a short time after, in which the landlord class and colonial garrison is revealed as the true beast of prey stalking the land [Fig. 11].

Fig. 11 'The English Vampire', *The Irish Pilot*, 7 November 1885

That this motif of the parasitic colonial administration persisted into the decade of Stoker's own composition of *Dracula* is clear from the vivid frontispiece to WT Stead's vigorous polemic, *The Centenary of 1798, and its bearing on the Practical Politics of Today* (1898) [Fig. 12].[114] The vampire this time is portrayed as a bloodthirsty eagle sinking its fangs into the prostrate body of an Irish peasant evicted from his thatched cabin – under, once again, the influence of moonlight.

Though the Gothic invocation of the supernatural points to breaches of the natural order, the true violation of nature involves attempts to press society itself, and hierarchies of power and domination, into a biological mould. It is through the Gothic that race is connected to the paranoid imagination, seeing in every member of a different society or religion a potential source of terror, which is all the more insidious for presenting itself as normal, or availing of the achievements of western society – freedom, market relations, mobility, education, technology.

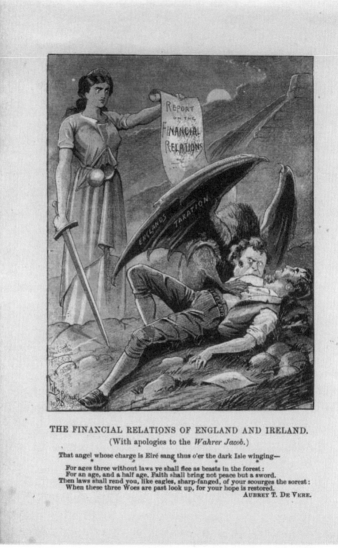

Fig. 12 'The Financial Relations of England and Ireland'

The possibility that these may act as a disguise for barely concealed forces of savagery and destruction is consistently applied to the alien or the immigrant, but is seldom conceded in relation to western modernity itself and the forced march of history. In his sociohistorical study of the Gothic and the 'fantastic' in literature, *A Spectre is Haunting Europe*, José Monleon points to a fundamental ambiguity in Goya's famous print, 'The Sleep of Reason', which shows a writer slumbering at his desk while strange vulpine and bat-like creatures hover menacingly overhead, casting dark shadows in the background. One interpretation of this accords with the received Enlightenment view: when reason sleeps, monsters awake. But as the composition and the structure of the image indicate, it is not so clear that the world of monsters is of a different order than that of the sleeper and his written page:

> Instead of articulating a gesture of exclusion, [Goya's print] suggests that there is indeed some continuity between the realms of reason and unreason, the latter being, in fact, a creation or product of the former ... By establishing a relation of cause and effect between reason and unreason Goya did more than simply recognize the coexistence of opposites. He was in fact proposing that the horizons of order created the threat of disorder, that the bourgeois world actually produced its own menacing monsters.[115]

For Monleon, the nineteenth-century literary imagination charts a course from the Gothic to 'the fantastic', in which the source of danger to civility passes from the outside – the outskirts of the city or the countryside – to within the confines of the city itself:

> The seeds of destruction – which the Gothic had always portrayed as coming from the margins of order – were accepted by the new industrial epoch as sown within its premises ... Just as the Gothic's tendency was to represent medieval and 'backward' settings, the new scenery in

popular literature became, especially after 1848, the 'unknown country' of the *bas-fonds*. (62-3)

The difficulty with this formulation is that the modern city is considered as self-contained, as if the various traces of the Gothic, and the appellations of 'savagery', 'barbarism', and so on, to the dangerous classes, are simply throwbacks to a bygone era. In fact, as Goya's print suggests, the two co-existed in the same urban space, and the Gothic itself was part of the present. English or American cities may have no longer felt threatened by their surrounding hinterlands but, as we have seen, they were not immune from the Irish countryside, from the pauperized hordes who crowded into the dens and filthy basements of the city backstreets. Monleon notes that over a century, the image of a city under siege from external threats gave way to alternative metaphors of cancer and disease emanating from within, but fails to add that the moral panic over disease had a *racial* as well as a class dimension, deriving also from an external source of contagion – the choleric Irish – which had infiltrated the city. Like the demons of Goya's print, moreover, these were not archaic feudal remnants but were monsters of its own making, as intrinsic to the operation of colonial modernity as the engines that drove the Industrial RevolutionCommenting on Saint-Marc Girardin's description of the social upheavals in Paris in 1831, that 'the barbarians who menace society are neither in the Caucasus nor in the steppes of Tartary; they are in the suburbs of our industrial cities', Monleon observes:

> Saint-Marc Girardin was deconstructing ... the metaphor of marginality, stressing the discovery of unreason *within the frame of order*, as if the masking undertaken by the Gothic had been not only inappropriate but also deceitful. (64)

But the Gothic had already addressed itself to the 'unreason within the frame of order', or at least that version of the Gothic launched by Burke, which sought to expose the dark side of modernity exemplified by Puritan righteousness, and its later racial, Teutonic expressions. Under the disciplinary regimes of this zealous modernity, those who persisted in the delusions of the pre-modern – through overheated imaginations, superstition, or collecti

e contagion – were removed to the new 'houses of confinement' that sprung up the edges of cities, as if to ward off the evils of outlying, primitive regions. In Maturin's *Melmoth the Wanderer*, one such asylum becomes the habitation of the unfortunate Englishman, Stanton, who sets out to track down the mysterious Melmoth during the Restoration period, only to find himself in company that harks back to the sectarian zeal of the Cromwellian conquest:

> Just next to Stanton's apartment were lodged two most uncongenial neighbours. One of them was a puritan weaver, who had been driven mad by a single sermon from the celebrated Hugh Peters, and was sent to the mad house as full of election and reprobation as he could hold – and fuller. He regularly repeated over the *five points* while day-light lasted, and imagined himself preaching in a conventicle with considerable success; towards twilight his visions were more gloomy, and at midnight his blasphemies became horrible.[116]

Next to godliness may be cleanliness, but in the eyes of Hugh Peters and his successors, ethnic cleansing was even nearer to God. If, as Leslie Fiedler attests, the Gothic typically recounts the story of someone 'who begins by looking for guilt in others and ends finding it in himself',[117] then the genre seems uniquely appropriate to capture the anomalies presented by Irishness to the racial Gothic of colonialism. What starts out as being strange and remote – over there, back then – ends up as being all too familiar, the nightmare produced by the dogmatic slumbers within oneself.

NOTES

[1] *Mr. Peters Last Report of the English Wars* (London: H Overton, 1646), 5. For comments on these sentiments of Peters, see Alden T Vaughan, *Roots of American Racism: Essays on the Colonial Experience* (Oxford: New York, 1995), 42; and Christopher Hill. '"Going Native": "The Noble Savage"', in *Liberty Against the Law: Some Seventeenth-Century Controversies* (London: Allen Lane/Penguin, 1996), 150.

[2] Vaughan, 42.

[3] Edmund Spenser, *A Breife Note of Ireland* [1598-9], cited in Theodore Allen, *The Invention of the White Race: Racial Oppression and Control* (London: Verso, 1994), 63, 210.

[4] See, for example, Peters's account of his own participation in the slaughter that accompanied the pacification of Munster in *A True Relation of the Passages of God's Providence in a Voyage for Ireland* (London: H Overton, 1642). For more on Peters, see Raymond Phineas Stearns, *The Strenuous Puritan: Hugh Peters, 1588-1660* (Urbana: University of Illinois Press, 1954), and AL Rowse, *Four Caroline Portraits: Thomas Hobbes, Henry Marten, Hugh Peters, John Selden* (London: Duckworth, 1993).

[5] See EJ Clery and Robert Miles, *Gothic Documents: A Sourcebook 1700-1820* (Manchester: Manchester University Press, 2000), 1-3.

[6] For a rejoinder to Colley's displacement of domestic and internal factors in the forging of Britishness, see Colin Kidd, *British Identities before Nationalism: Ethnicity and Nationhood in the Atlantic World, 1600-1800* (Cambridge: Cambridge University Press, 1999), chapters 9-10.

[7] David Armitage, *The Ideological Origins of the British Empire* (Cambridge: Cambridge University Press, 2000). Warning his son Henry about the barbarians of the Highland and Northern Isles, 'without any shew of civilitie', James IV recommended 'planting Colonies among them of answerable In-lands subjects, that within short time may reform and civilize the best among them; rooting out or transporting the barbarous or stubborn sort, and planting civilitie in their rooms', 56.

[8] L Perry Curtis, *Apes and Angels: The Irishman in Victorian Caricature*, revised edition (Washington: Smithsonian Institution Press, 1997), 115.

[9] See Joep T Leerssen, 'Wildness, Wilderness, and Ireland: Medieval and Early-Modern Patterns in the Demarcation of Civility', *Journal of the History of Ideas* (1995), 33.

[10] George Stocking, *Victorian Anthropology* (New York, Free Press, 1987), 234, cited in HL Malchow, *Gothic Images of Race in Nineteenth Century Britain* (Stanford: Stanford University Press, 1996), 70.

11 Malchow, 70.

12 *Punch*, XXIII (1848), 82, cited in Ned Lebow, 'British Historians and Irish History', *Éire-Ireland* vol. 7, no. 4, (Winter 1973), 11.

13 For the notion of an Irish 'spiritual empire' and its relation to prevailing colonial ideology, see Fiona Bateman, ' "The Spiritual Empire": Irish Catholic Missionary Discourse in the Twentieth Century', PhD Dissertation, NUI, Galway, 2003.

14 For the Gothic elements in Burke, see Siobhan Kilfeather, 'Origins of the Irish Female Gothic', *Bullán: An Irish Studies Journal* vol. 1, no. 2 (Autumn 1994), 35-47; Seamus Deane, *Strange Country: Modernity and Nationhood in Irish Writing Since 1790* (Oxford: Clarendon Press, 1997), chapter 1; Conor Cruise O'Brien, 'Introduction' to his edition of *Reflections on the Revolution in France* (Harmondsworth: Penguin, 1968), 31; Ronald Paulson, *Representations of Revolution* (New Haven: Yale University Press, 1983), chapters 3, 7; and Mary Jean Corbett, *Allegories of Union* (Cambridge: Cambridge University Press, 2000), chapter 1.

15 Edmund Burke, *Reflections on the Revolution in France* [1790], ed. JCD Clark (Stanford: Stanford University Press, 2001), 156-7.

16 Rolf Loeber and Magda Stouthammer-Loeber, 'The Publication of Irish Novels and Novelettes, 1750-1829: A Footnote on Irish Gothic Fiction', *Cardiff Corvey: Reading the Romantic Text* 10 (June 2003). Internet <http://www.cf.ac.uk/encap/corvey/articles/cc10_n02.html. 24/9/03. This article provides an invaluable bibliography of early Irish Gothic fiction.

17 Henry Fielding, *Tom Jones* [1747], ed. RPC Mutter (Harmondsworth: Penguin, 1970), 757-8. For a discussion of Garrick's playing of Hamlet in relation to both *Tom Jones* and the rise of the Gothic, see EJ Clery, *The Rise of Supernatural Fiction 1762-1800* (Cambridge: Cambridge University Press, 1995), 38-46.

18 See John Allen Stevenson's perceptive discussion, '*Tom Jones*, Jacobitism, and the Rise of the Gothic', in Allan Lloyd Smith and Victor Sage, eds., *Gothick Origins and Innovations* (Amsterdam: Rodopi, 1994), 16-22.

19 Robert Miles, 'Europhobia: the Catholic Other in Horace Walpole and Charles Maturin', in Avril Horner, ed., *European Gothic: A Spirited Exchange 1760-1960* (Manchester: Manchester University Press, 2002), 95.

20 As Colin Kidd argues, Gothicism in its previous Northern European political variant and Celticism represented different (though often convergent) genealogies of the peoples of Britain and Ireland. It is with the accession of the literary Gothic in the 1760s that the association with Celticism is given a new cultural valence (Kidd, chapter 8).

21 Kilfeather, 37.

22 April Alliston traces the theme of the Scottish Highlands as a setting for the spectacle of suffering feminine virtue central to the Gothic in Sophie von La Roche's *Geschichte des Frauleins von Sternheim* (1771) and Madame de Stael's *Corinne* (1807), as well as Sophia Lee's *The Recess*. April Alliston, 'The Haunted

Highlands: Mapping a Geography of Gender in the Margins of Europe', in Gregory Maertz, ed., *Cultural Interactions in the Romantic Age: Critical Essays in Comparative Literature* (Albany: State University of New York Press, 1998).

[23] TM Devine, *The Scottish Nation 1700-2000* (London: Penguin, 2000), 234. For a later critical exchange on the propriety of an overtly Scottish *Macbeth*, see the discussion of Ann Radcliffe's 'On the Supernatural in Poetry' below.

[24] Rupert Davenport-Hines, *Gothic: Four Hundred Years of Excess, Horror and Ruin* (London: Fourth Estate, 1998), 77-83, 94-6.

[25] Matthew Arnold, *On the Study of Celtic Literature, and Other Essays* [1867] (London: JM Dent, N.D.), 85.

[26] Sir Walter Scott, 'Introduction', *Rob Roy*, ed. Ian Duncan (Oxford: Oxford University Press, 1998), 5.

[27] Ian Duncan, 'Introduction', 15.

[28] John Pinkerton, *An Enquiry into the History of Scotland preceding the Reign of Malcom IIII, together with a Dissertation on the History of the Goths*, 2 vols. (Edinburgh: James Ballantyne, 1814), 184.

[29] Charles Maturin, *The Milesian Chief, A Romance* (London: H Colburn, 1812), v.

[30] William Shakespeare, *Hamlet*, ed. TJB Spencer, i, 5 (Penguin, 1980), 94.

[31] Steven Greenblatt, *Hamlet in Purgatory* (Princeton: Princeton University Press, 2001), 73-101, 229-37. Greenblatt's sustained analysis represents a considerable advance on A Bronson Feldman's earlier suggestion that the reason Hamlet swears by Ireland's national saint is that the action is taking place on St Patrick's Day, 17 March – and, even more unlikely, that Shakespeare may have been writing it on that day ('The March of Hamlet', *Shakespeare Newsletter*, December, 1963). In fact, St Patrick's Day was not officially recognized until the mid-seventeenth century, and was culturally marked for the first time by a parade in Boston in 1737.

[32] As Greenblatt points out, Hamlet's retort that the restless ghost is *'hic et ubique'* ('here and everywhere') draws on a phrase specifically connected to Catholic beliefs relating to purgatory that the soul of the departed is both imprisoned in one place, and condemned to roam the earth, 234-5.

[33] See Thomas Hobbes, *Leviathan*, ed. Richard Tuck (Cambridge: Cambridge University Press, 1991), 34 –36, 46.

[34] Daniel Brevint, *Saul and Samuel of Endor, or the New Waies of Salvation and Service, which usually Tem[p] t Men to Rome, and Detain them there, Truly Represented and Refuted* (Oxford: At The Theatre, 1679).

[35] James Macpherson, 'A Dissertation Concerning the Era of Ossian', in *The Poems of Ossian*, translated [sic] by James Macpherson, vol. ii (Dublin: J Moore, 1790), 170.

[36] Macpherson, 168, 170.

[37] William Collins, 'An Ode on the Popular Superstitions of the Highlands of Scotland, Considered as the Subject of Poetry', in Clery and Miles, eds., *Gothic Documents*, 46.

[38] Peter Womack, *Improvement and Romance: Constructing the Myth of the Highlands* (London: Macmillan, 1989), 91-93. Womack also cites William Duff's *Essay on Original Genius* (1767) in this respect: 'By the vigorous effort of a creative imagination, he [i.e. the poetic genius] calls shadowy substances and unreal objects into existence. They are present to his view, and glide, like spectres, before his astonished and entranced sight. In reading the descriptions of such apparitions, we partake of the Author's emotion; the blood runs chill in our veins, and our hair stiffens in horror.' (92). For a discussion of how the mediation of the experience of the supernatural through a third party – a character on the stage such as Garrick's Hamlet, or a character in fiction – facilitates a disturbing aesthetic effect, see Clery, *The Supernatural in Fiction*, 37-49.

[39] Collins, 'Ode on the Popular Superstitions', 45.

[40] Ann Radcliffe, 'On the Supernatural in Poetry', in Clery and Miles, eds., *Gothic Documents*, 164-5.

[41] Michel Foucault, *Discipline and Punish: The Birth of the Prison*, trans. Alan Sheridan (Harmondsworth: Penguin, 1981).

[42] Sigmund Freud, 'The Uncanny', *Works*, vol. 17, cited in Monleon, *A Spectre is Haunting Europe* (Princeton: Princeton University Press, 1994), 13.

[43] Adapted from Winthrop D Jordan, *White over Black: American Attitudes Toward the Negro 1550-1812* (Baltimore, MD: Penguin, 1969), 220-1.

[44] Jacques Le Goff, *The Birth of Purgatory*, trans. Arthur Goldhammer (Chicago: University of Chicago Press, 1981), 198-9.

[45] See Leerssen, 'Wildness, Wilderness, and Ireland', n. 9 above.

[46] Immanuel Kant, 'Of the Different Human Races', trans. Jon Mark Mikkelsen, in Robert Bernasconi and Tommy L. Lott, eds., *The Idea of Race* (Indianapolis: Hackett, 2000), 9-10. This did not prevent Kant from valourizing the German blond type as the ideal specimen of humanity.

[47] Johann Friedrich Blumenbach, 'On the Natural Variety of Mankind' [1795 edn.], trans. Thomas Bennyshe, in Bernasconi and Lott, eds., *The Idea of Race*, 31.

[48] Bruce Dain, *A Hideous Monster of the Mind: American Race Theory in the Early Republic* (Cambridge, MA: Harvard University Press, 2002), 23-6.

[49] Thomas Jefferson, 'Notes on the State of Virginia' (1781-2) in *Thomas Jefferson: Writings* (New York: Library of America, 1984), 197, 186, 264-5.

[50] Blumenbach, 'On the Natural Variety of Mankind', 33.

[51] Ronald T Takaki, *Iron Cage: Race and Culture in Nineteenth-Century America* (London: Athlone Press, 1980), 31.

[52] For concise critical discussions of the Nazi equation of Jews with disease and plague, and its implications for racial hygiene, see Zymunt Bauman, *Modernity and the Holocaust*, chapter 2; and Arno Mayer, *Why did the Heavens not Darken? The Final Solution in History* (London: Verso, 1990), 92-107, 342-3.

[53] Matthew Frye Jacobson, *Whiteness of a Different Colour: European Immigrants and the Alchemy of Race* (Cambridge, MA: Harvard University Press, 1998), chapters 1-3.

[54] Blumenbach, 'The Degeneration of Race' (excerpted from *On the Natural Varieties of Mankind*), in Emmanuel Chukwudi Eze, ed., *Race and the Enlightenment: A Reader* (London; Blackwell, 1997), 86.

[55] John Pinkerton, *An Enquiry into the History of Scotland*, vol. 1, 49.

[56] John Pinkerton, *A Dissertation on the Origin and Progress of the Scythians or Goths* (1794 edn), 123, cited in William Ferguson, *The Identity of the Scottish Nation: An Historic Quest* (Edinburgh: Edinburgh University Press, 1998), 253.

[57] JA Froude, *The English in Ireland in the Eighteenth Century* (London: Longman, 1887), 6, 12-3.

[58] Cited in Mary J Hickman, *Religion, Class and Identity: The State, the Catholic Church and the Education of the Irish in Britain* (London: Avebury, 1995), 186

[59] Samuel Taylor Coleridge, *The Courier*, December 1814, in *Essays on his Times*, ed. David Erdman (London: Princeton University Press, 1978), ii, 394, 405, 407, 409.

[60] Jacobson, 46.

[61] Chadwick Report: Liverpool [1840], cited in Frank Neal, *Black '47: Britain and the Famine Irish* (London: Macmillan, 1998), 26.

[62] James Philips Kay, *The Moral and Physical Conditions of the Working Classes Employed in the Cotton Manufacture in Manchester* (London: 1832), cited in Neal, 27.

[63] Kay, 28-9. Kay's importance in linking the Irish, race and epidemiology is noted in Graham Davis, 'Little Irelands' in Roger Swift and Sheridan Gilley, eds. *The Irish in Britain 1815-1939* (Savage, MD: Barnes and Noble, 1989), and is central to Mary Poovey's incisive study, *Making a Social Body: British Cultural Formation* (Chicago: University of Chicago, 1995), chapter 3.

[64] Bauman, 71, 59, 45, 58.

[65] Klaus Theweleit, *Male Fantasies*, vol. 2, trans. Erica Carter and Chris Turner (Minneapolis: University of Minnesota Press, 1989), 3-20.

[66] Thomas Carlyle, 'Chartism' [1839], in *English and other Critical Essays* (London: Dent, 1964), 183. For an outstanding discussion of Carlyle's 'epidemiology' of Ireland, see Amy Martin, 'Acts of Union: Representing Nation-States and National Identities in Victorian British and Irish Writing', PhD Dissertation, Columbia University, 2002, chapter 1.

[67] Thomas Carlyle, 'On Repeal of the Union' [1848], 31-2, cited in Martin, 95-6.

[68] RF Foster, 'Paddy and Mr Punch', in *Paddy and Mr Punch: Connections in Irish and English History* (London: Allen Lane/Penguin, 1993), 192.

[69] See, for example, Susan Thorne, ' "The Conversion of Englishmen and the Conversion of the World Inseparable": Missionary Imperialism and the Language of Class in Early Industrial Britain', in Frederick Cooper and Ann

Laura Stoller, eds., *Tensions of Empire: Colonial Cultures in a Bourgeois World* (Berkeley: University of California Press, 1997); and Christopher Herbert, *Culture and Anomie: Ethnographic Imagination in the Nineteenth Century* (Chicago: University of Chicago Press, 1991), especially chapter 4, 'Mayhew's Cockney Polynesia'.

70 See Richard Slotkin's magisterial discussion of the ideological re-working of class conflict in terms of the savagery of the frontier, *The Fatal Environment: The Myth of the Frontier in the Age of Industrialization 1800-1890* (New York: HarperPerennial, 1994). For the racialization of the Molly Maguires in these terms, see Slotkin, chapters 15, 18, 19, 20; Kevin Kenny, *Making Sense of the Molly Maguires* (New York: Oxford University Press, 1998), chapters 8, 9, and below.

71 Thorne, 247-8.

72 Catherine Hall, 'Rethinking Imperial Histories: The Reform Act of 1867', *New Left Review* 208 (November/December, 1994), 22-3.

73 Edmund Burke to Rev Thomas Hussey, post 9 December 1796, in TW Copeland, ed., *The Correspondence of Edmund Burke* (Cambridge: Cambridge University Press, 1970), vol. ix, 166; Rev. Thomas Hussey to Richard Burke, 28 August 1790, *Correspondence*, vi, 134.

74 Edmund Burke, *A Philosophical Enquiry into the Sublime and Beautiful* [1757], JT Boulton, ed., (London: Routledge and Kegan Paul, 1958), 175, 82.

75 George Cornewall Lewis, *Local Disturbances in Ireland* [1836] (Cork: Tower Books, 1977), 70

76 For Burke's family connections to the Whiteboys, see my *Edmund Burke and Ireland: Aesthetics, Politics and the Colonial Sublime* (Cambridge: Cambridge University Press, 2003), chapters 1, 5.

77 Tadhg O'Sullivan, ' "The Violence of Servile War": Three narratives of Irish Rural Insurgency post-1798', in Laurence M Geary, ed., *Rebellion and Remembrance in Modern Ireland* (Dublin: Four Courts Press, 2001), 79.

78 Cited in Charles Townsend, *Political Violence in Ireland: Government and Resistance since 1848* (Oxford: Oxford University Press, 1984), 17. For a similar description in the eighteenth century of a rapid spread of agrarian unrest which extended beyond local boundaries to grip the countryside at large, see Thomas Campbell's report of Oakboy activity in 1764: 'the discontent being as general as the grievance, the contagion seized the neighbouring parishes. From parishes it flew to baronies, and from baronies to counties, till at length the greater part of the province was engaged'. Campbell, *A Philosophical Survey of Ireland* (Dublin 1777), cited in Cornewall Lewis, *Local Disturbances*, 26

79 Patrick Geoghegan, *Robert Emmet: A Life* (Dublin: Gill and Macmillan, 2002), 81, 85.

80 Charles Maturin, *Melmoth the Wanderer* [1820] (Harmondsworth: Penguin, 1977), 343 (subsequent references in parentheses in text).

81 See Breandán MacSuibhne, 'Politicization and Paramilitarism: North-west and South-west Ulster, c1772-98', in Thomas Bartlett, David Dickson, Daire

Keogh, and Kevin Whelan, eds., *1798: A Bicentenary Perspective* (Dublin: Four Courts Press, 2003), 267-8.

[82] Fiona Robertson, *Legitimate Histories: Scott, Gothic, and the Authorities of Fiction* (Oxford: Clarendon Press, 1994), 105-6.

[83] Miles, 'Europhobia', 86. In an acute analysis, Miles proceeds to trace this spectre of Protestant terror in what he correctly identifies as the latent Irish nationalism of Charles Maturin's Gothic fiction. As we have seen, however, what for Hume is *internal* fanaticism, erring on the side of liberty, becomes for Burke and Maturin in an Irish context an *external* colonial imposition, depriving the mass of the population of their liberty.

[84] David Hume, 'Of Superstition and Enthusiasm' [1741], in Richard Wollheim, ed., *Hume on Religion* (London: Fontana, 1968), 250.

[85] Edmund Burke, 'Letter to Richard Burke', *Works*, Bohn Standard Library (London: George Bell, 1901), vi, 75.

[86] Burke, 'Letter to Richard Burke', 77.

[87] Maturin, *The Milesian Chief*, 52, 62.

[88] Hume, 'Of Superstition and Enthusiasm', 249.

[89] There is little doubt that a similar upwardly mobile identification of the Irish with whiteness in the United States militated against solidarity with those on the lowest rung of the labour market – African-Americans in the east or, on the west coast, Chinese immigrants. Yet, as Matthew Frye Jacobson demonstrates, immigrant status itself and the barriers of anti-Catholicism and anti-Celticism made this more problematic than the sharing of a dominant 'common' culture (as in the case of the British working class). The persistence of the hegemonic WASP element within whiteness produced conflicting modes of assimilation, one in which the Irish tried to be more white and patriotic than the Americans themselves (through, for example, military service, Catholic led anti-Communism campaigns, or, indeed, espousals of racism), and the other hand, a radical counter-current, promoted by Irish labour activists such as Patrick Ford or civil liberterians like John Boyle O'Reilly, that encouraged cross-ethnic rather than cross-class alliances, establishing new modes of solidarity with other immigrant groups, blacks, and native Americans. See Matthew Frye Jacobson, *Special Sorrows; The Diasporic Imagination of Irish, Polish and Jewish Immigrants in the United States* (Cambridge, MA: Harvard University Press, 1995).

[90] Margot Finn, *After Chartism: Class and Nation in English Radical Politics, 1848-1874* (Cambridge: Cambridge University Press, 1993), 186-7.

[91] Karl Marx, 'From the Federal Council to the General Council of French Switzerland' [1870], in Karl Marx and Frederick Engels, *Articles on Britain* (Moscow: Progress Publishers, 11971), 357, 356-7.

[92] Frederick Engels, *The Condition of the Working Class in England* [1845] (London: Panther, 1976), 298. Subsequent references in parentheses in text.

[93] John Plotz, *The Crowd: British Literature and Public Politics* (Berkeley: University of California Press, 2000), 137-9. As Carlyle expressed it in

'Chartism': 'Chartist torch-meetings, Birmingham riots, Swing conflagrations, are so many symptoms on the surface; you abolish the symptom to no purpose, if the disease is left untouched. Boils on the surface are curable or incurable, – small matter which, while the virulent humour festers deep within; poisoning the sources of life; and certain enough to find for itself ever new boils and sore issues' (cited in Plotz, 144). As we shall see below, it is not incidental to Carlyle's rhetoric that the leadership, and much of the militancy, of the Chartist movement was in Irish hands.

94 Dr Isaac Taylor, *The Origin of the Aryans: An Account of the Prehistoric Ethnology and Civilisation of Europe* [1889], cited in JM Robertson, *The Saxon and the Celt: A Study in Sociology* (London: University Press, 1897), 93. Robertson's sustained assault on Victorian racism deserves to be better known, particularly among those inclined to exonerate British imperial precursors of Aryan race theory for following 'the spirit of the age', as if there was no access to cultural or historical alternatives to biological models.

95 Donald Read and Eric Glasgow, *Feargus O'Connor: Irishman and Chartist* (London: Edward Arnold, 1961), 75-6

96 Coleridge, *The Courier*, 9-10 December 1814, in *Essays on our Times*, 411-14.

97 Plotz, 132.

98 Hence, notwithstanding his explicit renunciations of violence, the prosecution and imprisonment of Daniel O'Connell for concealed seditious designs behind his monster meeeting and modes of political mobilization. For a discussion of the paranoid style informing the prosecution, see my 'Republicanism and Radical Memory: The O'Conors, O'Carolan, and the United Irishmen', in Jim Smyth, ed., *Revolution, Counter-Revolution and the Union* (Cambridge: Cambridge University Press, 2000).

99 John Belcham, *Popular Radicalism in Nineteenth-Century Britain* (London: St Martin's Press, 1996), 91-3.

100 I discuss this earlier example of racial Gothic in 'Ireland, America and Gothic Memory: Transatlantic Terror in the Early Republic', *Boundary 2*, special Irish Studies issue (Spring 2004).

101 Cited in *The Unknown Power behind the Irish Nationalist Party: Its Present Work and Criminal History*, ed. The Right Hon Lord Ashtown (London: Swan Sonnenchein/ Offices of 'Grievance from Ireland', 1908), 114-16. Gowan allegedly expressed these alarms to Allan Pinkerton, head of the detective agency employed to track down the Mollies, who subsequently recorded them in his 'most romantic and truthful' memoir, *The Molly Maguires and the Detectives*.

102 Sir Arthur Conan Doyle, *The Valley of Fear*, ed. Owen Dudley Edwards (Oxford: Oxford University Press, 1993), 6. Subsequent references in parentheses in text.

[103] Max Nordau, *Degeneration* (London: Heineman, 1895), 22, cited in Catherine Wynne, *The Colonial Conan Doyle: British Imperialism, Irish Nationalism and the Gothic* (Westport, CT: Greenwood Press, 2002), 58.

[104] Wynne, 48.

[105] Bram Stoker, *Personal Reminiscences of Henry Irving*, i, (London: Heinemann, 1906), 344.

[106] Joseph Valente, *Dracula's Crypt: Bram Stoker, Irishness, and the Question of Blood* (Urbana: University of Chicago Press, 2002), 61.

[107] Bram Stoker, *Dracula*, ed. Nina Auerbach and David J. Skal (New York: Norton, 1997), 26.

[108] Valente, 59, 60, 71.

[109] Stoker, *Dracula*, 41

[110] Bram Stoker, College Historical Society: Address Delivered . . . 13 November 1872 (Dublin: James Charles and So, 1872), 29-30. For discussions of Stoker's Address, see Chris Morash, ' "Ever Under some Unnatural Condition": Bram Stoker and the Colonial Fantastic', in Brian Cosgrove, ed., *Literature and the Supernatural* (Dublin: The Columba Press, 1995), 100-5, and Valente, *Dracula's Crypt*, 21-7.

[111] *The Tomahawk*, 7 August 1869.

[112] *Punch*, 24 October 1885.

[113] See, for example, Morash, 'Ever Under some Unnatural Condition', 110ff.; Michael Moses, 'Dracula, Parnell and the Troubled Dreams of Nationhood', *Journal X: A Journal in Culture and Criticism*, vol. 2, no. 1 (Autumn 1997); Cannon Schmitt, *Alien Nation* (Philadelphia: University of Pennsylvania Press, 1997); Bruce Stewart, 'Bram Stoker's *Dracula*: Possessed by the Spirit of the Nation?', *Irish University Review*, vol. 29, no. 2 (Autumn/Winter 1999).

[114] WT Stead , *The Centenary of 1798, and its Bearing on the Practical Politics of Today* (London: 'Review of Reviews' Office, 1898).

[115] Monleon, 41-2. Subsequent references in parentheses in text.

[116] Maturin, 92-3.

[117] Leslie Fiedler, *Love and Death in the American Novel* (Paladin, 1970), 148.